The Doctoral Thesis Journey

Reflections from Travellers and Guides

THE THURSDAY GROUP

Edited by Ardra L. Cole and David E. Hunt

The Ontario Institute for Studies in Education

The Ontario Institute for Studies in Education has three prime functions: to conduct programs of graduate study in education, to undertake research in education, and to assist in the implementation of the findings of educational studies. The Institute is a college chartered by an Act of the Ontario Legislature in 1965. It is affiliated with the University of Toronto for graduate studies purposes.

The publications program of the Institute has been established to make available information and materials arising from studies in education, to foster the spirit of critical inquiry, and to provide a forum for the exchange of ideas about education. The opinions expressed should be viewed as those of the contributors.

Canadian Cataloguing in Publication Data
Main entry under title:

The Doctoral thesis journey : reflections of
travellers and guides

(Monograph ; 27)
Includes bibliographical references.
ISBN 0-7744-0415-9

1. Ontario Institute for Studies in Education —
Dissertations. 2. Dissertations, Academic — Ontario —
Toronto. 3. Doctor of education degree. 4. Degrees,
Academic —Ontario – Toronto. 5. Education —
Research — Ontario — Toronto. 6. Ontario Institute
for Studies in Education — Graduate students.
7. Ontario Institute for Studies in Education —
Faculty. I. Cole, Ardra Linette, 1953-   .
II. Hunt, David E., 1925-   . III. Series:
Monograph series (Ontario Institute for Studies in
Education) ; 27.

LB1742.D63 1994   370'.7'309713541   C94-930633-9

Cover Design: Helmut W. Weyerstrahs

ISBN 0-7744-0415-9   Printed in Canada
1 2 3 4 5 6 HP 99 89 79 69 59 49

To Seymour B. Sarason
with
appreciation and affection

Contents

Introduction

The Thursday Group

This book is a creation of the Thursday Group, so you need
to know a little about us. We are experienced professionals
in education — university faculty, consultants, school
administrators, ministry staff, etc. — who come together
for informal discussion, colleagueship, and a few laughs.
We have been meeting at OISE (The Ontario Institute for
Studies in Education) every other Thursday at noon for
over fifteen years.

Many of us work at OISE, others have received their
doctorates from OISE and now work elsewhere in other
universities, school boards, or private consultation, and
some of us have no connection with OISE. Since our more
formal title is the Educational Development Discussion
Group, we often talk about how to facilitate the teaching-
learning process. Sometimes, we plan a topic in advance,
but, more often, we allow whatever seems to be on our
minds to emerge for discussion. We have no formal principles, but there is one unexpressed belief which guides all
of our discussions: we speak from our own direct experience, not from theoretical models or abstractions. We may
consider some general points later, but our discussions are
always rooted in our own direct experience of teaching,
supervision, consultation, administration, or counselling.

Another regularity is the annual visit in the Spring by
Seymour Sarason who comes over from Yale University,
usually for our last meeting in April. His visit is always a

highlight, and, with this book, we reciprocate his many years of support and stimulation by dedicating it to him. This gift to Seymour comes from all members of the Thursday Group, past and present, whether their names appear here or not.

How this Book Came About

Last Spring, we spent a couple of Thursday meetings discussing the doctoral thesis process, a topic important for many of us, since several of us either supervise theses or have completed the thesis process in recent years. These discussions led to the observation that much of the inner process and the real work in completing a doctoral thesis has not been described in a way which would be available to future doctoral thesis students. Some Thursday Group colleagues who had spent a session with doctoral students describing their thesis process after completion, confirmed that students are hungry for information about what it is really like, since it is a totally new experience. So, the idea of demystifying the thesis process by writing about our own experiences was born. It would be from Inside-out, reflecting on our own experiences.

As we moved to consider putting together a book on the topic, the idea of viewing the thesis process as journey was proposed and greeted with enthusiastic approval. Thesis-as-journey offered many possibilities: considering the thesis student as traveller and the supervisor as guide, as well as providing a description of role reversal for each party, "If I were a guide" and "When I was a traveller," respectively.

With the understanding that it was to be a book by the Thursday Group, Ardra Cole and Dave Hunt agreed to be responsible for sending out specific instructions and deadlines, collecting and editing manuscripts, and sending completed manuscripts to publishers. The instructions were very brief, emphasizing that colleagues write personally about their actual experiences, with a minimum of bibliographic citation; a light-hearted approach to a heavy topic. They were specifically requested to include some "Tips to travellers" and to reverse their roles, i.e., "If I were a guide" for travellers and "When I was a traveller" for guides. Most authors reported that they enjoyed the writing and almost all of the reflections came in on time, an even more surprising outcome.

Doctoral Thesis Work at OISE

Since all of the guides and most of the travellers describe their experience at OISE, a few comments describing doctoral theses research at OISE seem appropriate. The zeitgeist (climate) for the kind of thesis research which is acceptable at OISE has changed dramatically in the past twenty years. In the sixties and early seventies, most theses were conducted, using the scientific paradigm of controlled experiments derived from a logico-deductive approach, the quantitative approach, if you will. Since then, an alternative to this traditional approach, variously called qualitative, phenomenological, heuristic or, simply non-traditional has been adopted as the guiding philosophical and methodological base, until it is now the rule rather than the exception. Specifically, OISE doctoral students have a choice of approaches and, if they choose the non-traditional, they can begin with themselves, use their own experience as a legitimate foundation for inquiry, write in the first person singular, etc.

This shift is mirrored by many of the reflections in this book, but we hope this does not mean that it applies only to doctoral students and faculty at OISE. For whatever the underlying epistemology and methodology, the doctoral thesis journey is an inner journey, with personal meaning for each traveller.

Educational Research in the Nineties

The past twenty years has also seen a similar shift in non-traditional or qualitative approaches in educational research settings throughout North America. Perhaps the best indicator of this dramatic shift can be seen in the program or journals of the AERA (American Educational Research Association), where qualitative approaches have become the rule rather than the exception, just as at OISE. Eliot Eisner's 1993 Presidential address to AERA is a case in point.

There is a curious contradiction in all this amazing shift. Up until the late 1960s, educational research was essentially the step-child of Mainstream Psychology, depending on it for its theories and especially for its methodology, which was the scientific method. Now that the shift described here has occurred and educational research seems to have asserted itself and set its own directions for acceptable inquiry, its former step-parent, Mainstream Psychology, seems to have changed very little and still emulates the traditional scientific model. We leave it to future historians of higher education to unravel this curious series of developments. For now, we state again that this does not mean that these reflections are only for educational researchers, we hope that they portray the thesis process in ways which may be meaningful to doctoral students and faculty in other disciplines.

Also, although we use the Canadian convention of referring to the doctoral thesis rather than the doctoral dissertation, we trust that this will not limit the meaning of the experiences described.

To the Reader

Although we did not plan it, this book turns out to exemplify non-traditional research. For example, there is no attempt at a representative or random sample of travellers or guides. Rather, there are nineteen personal reflections, which together form a composite portrait of the phenomenon. Some reflections may agree or even repeat what is in another reflection, while some may be in disagreement. Such agreement and contradiction are in the nature of the journey.

In addition to doctoral thesis students and faculty, we hope that these reflections may be of interest to those in the family of the thesis student. Perhaps these non-technical reflections may help communicate the complexities of the journey to the travellers' families.

The reflections are presented in alphabetical order, so feel free to dip in at any point to begin your own journey. Bon voyage!

The Thursday Group
December, 1993

Going Backwards and Other Reflections

William E. Alexander

> Thesis Title:
>
> **Some Sociological Aspects of Psychological Well-Being in a Schizophrenic Population: Social Class Participation and Work**
>
> Unpublished doctoral dissertation, Syracuse University, 1967.

A colleague advised me that when working to overcome my writing block (which is perpetually present) I should meditate on the topic. So, I began by meditating and then, as any good academic would do, I went to the dictionary.

First, a word on my meditation. The topic is "supervision" — kind of a strange word when you think about it. I always thought of super vision as a quality that Superman had — the simple ability to see through walls (except lead ones). When I was five years old I remember asking why Superman did not win the war for us. I was told that he had gone to take the army physical exam and when it came to reading the eye chart he accidentally read the chart in the next room. The doctor assumed he was blind as a bat and failed him. So poor Superman was stuck for the duration fighting crime in the streets. At least he was in uniform. So much for meditation. On to the dictionary.

Super: meaning, "over and above, superior, higher in quantity, quality or degree, exceeding a norm, surpassing all or most others of its kind or class as in power, size or complexity." Wow! And *vision:* meaning, "something seen otherwise than by the ordinary sight: an imaginary, supernatural or prophetic sight beheld in sleep or ecstasy; one that conveys a revelation" (Webster's 3rd International). Does this mean that we who supervise theses are supposed to be superior supernaturalists who spend a lot of time in sleep or ecstasy?   Seems reasonable to me.

Now that we have established the meaning of the term "supervision" let me tell you how it really works.

Going Backwards
February, 1968:

M. peeked into my office and, with a gentle rap on the door said, "Bill, do you mind if I come in and talk with you a minute?" "Come on in and have a seat," I replied, clearing books and papers off the chair closest to my desk.

"Well, Bill, I know you're not a member of my thesis committee but I'd like to talk to you about something that's happening. I need some advice."
"I'll do my best," I said.

M. leaned forward and in a near whisper told me, "I'm getting close to finishing my thesis. I have a draft all written and I submitted it to my committee. Yesterday I met with my committee and a strange thing happened." M. continued. "First, you should know that throughout this whole process my supervisor has been okay. I have no major complaints.   Both my supervisor and my committee have been, well, let's say, a hands off committee. I remember asking for advice a number of times early in the process and members would simply answer my questions with questions of their own. I found this extraordinarily frustrating at first but got over it."

M.'s voice grew agitated. "It was tough in those early days, two and a half years ago. I got no direction and had to do virtually everything myself. I was not prepared because my courses simply hadn't given me practice in doing a piece of research of this scope and depth. Nonetheless, I became a truly self-directed learner and got through it all. At least I thought I got through it all until yesterday."

M. sighed and continued. "The problem is this. For two and a half years my committee let me go on my own merry way. Now, I have given them the final chapters and there are all kinds of changes they want. I don't want to change anything and I don't think I should have to. If they wanted it done differently why didn't they say so two years ago when they got my proposal? I'm really frustrated and angry and I'm not sure what to do about it."

"What have they asked you to change?" I questioned.
M.'s eyes moved up and left, "Well, they want me to con-

duct a new kind of data analysis, read several new theorists and relate their work to my findings, make all kinds of changes in sentence structure and grammar and add a chapter about next steps."

This was a conversation I first heard in 1968 and then again in 1970, 1971, etc. It wasn't until 1978 that I was able to develop a coherent idea of what was happening. In 1978 I learned about a theory of supervision called Situational Leadership.

Situational Leadership

Situational Leadership (Hersey & Blanchard, 1982) has become the most popular theory of supervision in the world, and training in this style of supervision has occurred on all continents. Many believe its popularity is because the theory so accurately reflects both our experience and preferences in the subordinate-supervisor relationship. It says that there is no one perfect leadership style; rather, each common style is appropriate for certain situations but not for others.

Situational leadership has two interrelated models. The first is a developmental model of the stages subordinates go through as they learn to master a complex task. The second model proposes the optimum response from the supervisor at each stage. I will describe each of these models.

The theory of Situational Leadership states that a person with a task to complete goes through four stages. These stages can be characterized by the person's level of commitment and competence. In Stage one, the person is "full steam ahead" — highly committed although, as he or she will soon learn, low in competence. This stage certainly fits most thesis students who are engaging in a major research project for the first time in their lives. There is often a great deal of anxiety and a great deal of excitement and commitment as the student struggles to choose which of the two or three topics to focus on and then to narrow the problem to a manageable size.

Stage two represents the "honeymoon is over" period when the reality sets in that actually completing the complex task is not as easy as it seemed at first. In fact, it now seems extraordinarily difficult. Commitment drops to a very low point as dissatisfaction sets in but competence continues to improve as the person grapples with the variety of problems that must be solved in order to complete the task. This stage, too, seems like a fair description of many thesis students with whom I have spoken and worked. Often satisfaction is highest after the proposal is accepted and then, when the real work begins, satisfaction and commitment plummet to a very low level.

Stage three is a "nuts and bolts" stage as the person continues pushing through the process. The person is working away and all the time improving competence, although not necessarily feeling that way. At the same time, commitment is up and down, up and down. Each new insight brings a new high. A period of being stuck brings about depression and wondering why the thesis was started in the first place; however, no high is as high as the first high in Stage one and no low as low as the first low in Stage two.

Stage four is "Maturity." The subordinate finally recognizes that he or she is indeed high in competence. Commitment, as well, moves to a high level. Now there is a high degree of self-confidence with the recognition that the task can be completed in a very satisfactory manner. With thesis students Stage four is often evidenced by eagerness to get on with the next piece of research — a piece as complex as their doctoral thesis. When the student completes the thesis and asks the supervisor to write letters of recommendation for postdoctoral work, this is an indication that the student has landed in the centre of Stage four.

In the second model of Situational Leadership Blanchard (1984) proposes that a good supervisor recognize, actually "diagnose," the stage the subordinate is in and respond appropriately. Failure to respond appropriately can result in the subordinate remaining in a particular stage for a longer time than necessary which decreases efficiency. Or, the subordinate might become so dissatisfied that he or she will quit the job altogether. This diagnosis includes "reading" the subordinate's learning style in order to match the appropriate supervision strategy. As I discuss in this final section, thesis students vary greatly in their styles, and the journey goes more smoothly if both parties know and adapt to this style.

The supervisor has two major types of interventions available: task interventions (which focus on the content of the job) and process interventions (sometimes called support or maintenance interventions and often focussing on relationship issues). Interestingly, what is considered by the Situational Leadership model to be the most appropriate supervisory style is virtually antithetical to that practiced by most thesis supervisors. And, as I will explain, for very good reason.

Supervision and Situational Leadership

In Stage one, "full steam ahead," situational leadership theory prescribes that the supervisor take a very directive approach, focusing exclusively on task interventions by letting the subordinate know what to do, how to do it, and by providing role expectations, decision-making structures and other information relevant to fulfilling the task in the expected manner. One-way communication predominates. Not surprisingly, this is sometimes referred to as the *telling style* and in this stage the supervisor provides very low levels of support. In other words, there are few, if any, maintenance interventions.

In Stage two, when the "honeymoon is over," and the subordinate realizes that the thesis is simply a job and a pretty tough one at that, the situational leadership supervisor continues to provide a great deal of direction but now provides lots of support as well. The supervisor lets the subordinate understand how the work fits in a more general context. Or, using 1993 jargon, the supervisor might share the organization's vision with the subordinate in an effort to enroll the subordinate in that vision. This, it is believed, will provide a higher level of commitment. This supervisory style is sometimes referred to as the *selling style* or, in some versions of situational leadership, the *coaching style.*

As the subordinate continues to learn and develop, the supervisor switches to a *participating style* and involves the subordinate in a joint decision-making process. The supervisor reduces task interventions and keeps the process interventions high. Presumably, the idea is to acknowledge the subordinate's increasing level of competence and raise his or her self-esteem. Here, support is high and direction low; process interventions frequent and task interventions very infrequent.

Finally, the supervisor moves to a *delegating style* where he or she can withdraw both task and process interventions. Here the supervisor might simply state the outcomes required and let the subordinate take it from there.

There is low support and low direction in acknowledgment of the subordinate's expertise, autonomy and capacity to generate intrinsic rewards.

Practitioners of situational leadership who viewed the actual thesis process at work would conclude (rightly, in my view) that thesis supervisors do things backwards, particularly with respect to task interventions. This is mainly due to the unique design of the thesis exercise. The specifics of this uniqueness will be described below. Suffice it to point out here that most students and many academics fail to recognize that the supervision process is being played out in reverse. Understandably, students often feel confused and sometimes angry and betrayed.

A thesis student, of course, begins the thesis process in Stage one. A situational leadership supervisor would respond by providing high direction and little support. A thesis supervisor, however, provides very little direction. Instead, the supervisor treats the student as if the student is in Stage four; that is to say, the supervisor delegates. The supervisor and committee might ask questions for clarification and even criticize if the problem is not clear, or the methodology inappropriate. But they generally do not see their job as providing specific direction — an appropriate Stage one response under ordinary circumstances. In fact, most supervisors I know claim that one of the great errors a thesis supervisor can make is to provide the student with a thesis question. These supervisors advise their younger colleagues to "keep *your* questions to yourself."

Maybe some think that by giving a student a course in statistics and research methods and, nowadays, a course in qualitative research, we are preparing them for the tough task of writing a thesis; however, very few courses in graduate school ask students to conduct research, and most of the feedback students receive on their papers is of little use in honing their research skills. So, while students must begin their thesis with Stage four supervision, they generally have the maturity of someone in Stage one or two.

So, in the beginning of the thesis process the student finds that the supervisor is using a Stage four response — delegating. And, as the thesis nears completion and the student is in Stage four, feeling competent and committed, he or she is suddenly faced with a supervisor and committee using Stage one responses. The supervisor and committee members move to the telling style and begin giving the student directions. Some students complain that their supervisor and committee members are making outrageous demands, as M. did in my office in 1968. After months of independence, the student suddenly experiences a great deal of direction as the supervisor and committee tell the student what "tasks" to complete. Even if the supervisor and committee are supportive, many students become angry and confused. A few have told me that they felt "betrayed."

The system of accountability in normal jobs is from subordinate to supervisor. In the thesis process, however, the accountability system is substantially different. The final examination of a doctoral student includes the presence of an examiner from an external university. As the oral examination draws near, the supervisor and committee members begin to deal with *their* issues of identification. *They* begin to identify with the thesis. If the external examiner believes the thesis is a failure then that may also mean that the committee members and supervisor have failed to do their job. The supervisor may project the external examiner's thinking and imagine the appraisal stating: "How could this supervisor and this committee let such a shabby piece of work go forward to an oral? Clearly, the supervisor and committee must be absolutely incompetent."

I suspect that, in most cases, the demands for content changes are simply in service of a more adequate thesis document. If the supervisor is insecure, overly sensitive to criticism or brand new and naive about the process, then he or she may be particularly hard on the thesis student. The student is left with the complex task of protecting the reputation of the supervisor, the committee, the department and the university.

The student who is used to traditional supervisory practice had better prepare for a brand new supervisory experience — and learn to accept and work with backwards supervision. The faculty member might do well to let the student know that the supervisory relationship in a thesis context is significantly different than other supervisory relationships the student may have encountered. And, finally, academic departments might wish to consider if there is more they could do to help students develop the necessary thesis competencies prior to working with a thesis supervisor. This would, of course, make the transitions all the easier.

When I was a Traveller

I hated writing my thesis. Well, let us say that it was not my favourite activity. My real thesis never got written. I was told by my mentor that the proposal was great. All I had to do was to go back to graduate school for two years and study mathematics and I would be able to do the thesis. So far no one else has done the study. So I have this great thesis proposal if anyone is looking for one.

My PhD is in Sociology and, while I did take a little mathematics, I never did have the aptitude to learn math easily and integrate it into my everyday world. The particular branches of mathematics I needed were graph theory and linear algebra and I knew just enough about those areas to know that I was not about to return to graduate school for a second trip.

My second proposal was not bad either. It even got funded by the United States Department of Education. But then along came Vietnam and my funding was converted into part of a napalm bomb.

So, as I searched around, lost soul that I was, a former classmate came to my rescue. He had graduated the year before and was a senior researcher in a state Mental Health Research Unit. He gave me the opportunity to do a thesis on data collected by his project. He also offered me a modest salary, an office (together with office hours), the services of a secretary and a programmer. (This was 1966 and even the simplest of statistical tests took the specialized know-how of a programmer.) I happily accepted and began working in an area about which I knew absolutely nothing — mental health. The thesis just about ruined my own mental health. From the mass of data generated by the project, I chose to conduct a secondary analysis examining sociological correlates of psychological well-being in a schizophrenic population.

All this was happening in the late 1960s, the years of the "sellers' market." Graduates would have a half dozen really good job offers from which to choose. Universities would be happy to accept ABD's (all but dissertations) and give you some time to write it later on; however, I knew of many cases of fellow-students who had gone off into the life of a university teacher only to get overwhelmed with campus life. They put their theses on hold, some for five years, some for life. At that time I cannot say that I had any exceptional self-knowledge but I did recognize that discipline was not a quality I possessed in great abundance. And, I was sure that discipline was at least one of the major qualities needed to complete a thesis. So I made a bargain with myself. I said I would not leave the city where I was attending university until my thesis was written. Since I did not like living in that city this was kind of a pact with myself — finish my thesis and I give myself permission to get out of town.

My friend and colleague provided me with the perfect context. He gave me the structure which provided the focus for the discipline I needed in order to write the thesis. In addition, he was a tough taskmaster. He read a chapter at a time, critiqued it and sent it back. I owe this friend, colleague and taskmaster a great debt of gratitude, and if one could dedicate chapters in books to people I would most certainly dedicate this chapter to him.

It was not until much later that I realized how important, even critical, that structure was for me at that time in my life. Since I have now spent a number of years in a Department of Adult Education I have become aware of ideas like learning style and learning needs. So, now I invite all the students I supervise to reflect on their own style and needs and, if they want to, to develop a contract with me. They may want me to call once a month — "the nagging parent." Or, they may ask me to tell them how much it means to me personally to have them finish their thesis — "the guilt trip." Fortunately for me, no student has ever asked me to play roles like those mentioned above although several have reflected on their own style and told me the nature of their learning issues.

I have learned much about the thesis journey from my own experience as a traveller and as a guide. Several important things stand out.

- It is sometimes helpful for thesis students to get a good sense of their learning needs and spend some time designing, inventing or creating whatever is needed. They may know these needs before they begin or they may discover them as they move through the process. Either way, stay alert.

As I mentioned, one of the things I needed was some good solid structure. Maybe I would not have needed it so much if I were more intrinsically motivated. Perhaps things would have been different if I had been able to pursue one of my original topics.

- I also needed friends or colleagues with whom I could talk. Sometimes I simply needed to complain; sometimes I wanted to talk about a particular content issue related to the thesis. I was most fortunate to work with some brilliant and supportive people. So, I had both intellectual stimulation and assistance as well as emotional support.

- I have not talked about my oral defense and I will not, except to say that I had a basic misunderstanding. Somehow, I got confused about the terms "defense" and "defensive" and I entered with lots of the latter. I think I was frightened by the (mis)conception that if I conceded one point I would lose the whole contest. On the other hand, I also believed that if I fought with a member of the examining committee, he would fail me. Happily for me I was wrong on both counts. I now believe that when you believe you're right, fight (well gently). When you're wrong, concede. I now advise candidates to listen to the examiners as if they just might be right, reflect their statement or question back to them, take two deep breaths to get centred and respond. A few candidates have even taken my advice.

In an Outward Search Look Inward

Eleanor Allgood

Thesis Title:

Implicit Theories About Practice Become Explicit: Case Studies of School Counsellors' Experiences

Unpublished doctoral thesis, University of Toronto, 1990.[1]

Have you ever known that you wanted to understand something, perhaps something that you felt deeply about, but could not find the words to express it so that you could begin your search for meaning? This was the experience that started me on my doctoral thesis journey. The understanding that I was seeking focussed on my personal relation to my counselling practice. This desire grew out of an awareness that I brought some heart-felt beliefs to my practice yet I had difficulty expressing them to myself or to others with whom I worked. Knowing more about those undercurrents that shaped my practice became a driving force within me.

At the time I began my doctoral studies, I was a guidance counsellor in a high school and I was expressing the question that kept gnawing at me as something like — What is it about ourselves that we bring to our counselling practice that is important beyond our technique? Although I had few ideas of how to develop this question so that it would guide a thesis, as the time approached for me to decide on my thesis topic it became clear that somehow I was going to work with it. In the Spring of my residence

---

[1] Graduate studies at the Ontario Institute for Studies in Education (OISE) occur within the Graduate Department of Education at the University of Toronto; therefore, graduate degrees are granted by the University of Toronto, not from OISE.

year, I enrolled in a research methods class, and through
it I began to develop a proposal that focussed on guidance
counsellors expressing their personal knowledge in relation
to their work. One of the first steps any budding researcher
engages in is a literature search. I had always liked researching essays so I began my quest with a feeling of
pleasure and anticipation; however, unlike past experiences
I went down many blind alleys finding little that related
directly to this area. Feeling increasingly frustrated, I
pursued one lead after another to no avail. Then one day in
class, my teacher gave me an unpublished article on the
"personal" which opened a door for me and began my learning about personal knowledge and professional practice.
That unexpected and highly appropriate gift coming at just
the right moment, was the beginning of my eventual success in developing a proposal.

All the while I was feeling unclear about the exact form
and structure of my work. I did not yet know how to understand my question in ways that would enable me to create
a thesis project. The attendant problem was that if I could
not speak to my guide (supervisor) and potential committee
members about it in more detail, how could I hope to develop a proposal or a thesis? With more faith than anything else, I approached my guide (supervisor) and tried to
find adequate words to give him some real sense of my
question. It was my good fortune that he was a compassionate and intuitive man and, through our dialogue, I
began to create a vision of my work. Then he suggested
that since he was going on sabbatical (Was my new found
life rope to be jerked away so soon?), I could possibly benefit from talking to another professor who also might be a
potential guide (committee member). So, praying for another favorable reception, off I went to try out my new
words with him.

From the moment I began to speak about my idea this
man knew what I was talking about! In fact, he, himself,
was engaged in research on similar themes and offered me
articles to read and indicated that a new book, which he
was writing, could help me with my work. I had found a
common ground for understanding and a path on which to
begin my journey! I felt such relief and joy at finally being
able to proceed with a real sense of direction towards defining my work and posing my question in a research form.

From these tentative but progressive steps, I learned the

importance of sharing my thoughts and ideas as I developed and focussed them. Those meetings were the catalysts for my reflections about my work and the shape it would eventually take.

The activities described above all took place during my year of residency at the university. The rest of my work on my thesis was done while I was working full time and during the summer "vacation."

During my first year back at work, I developed the research design in consultation with my guide and obtained the co-operation of six guidance counsellors who agreed to be part of my study. We would begin to meet early in the Fall of the next year. Developing the design and creating the research experience were processes that went rather smoothly, albeit slowly, as I was deeply engaged in my counselling work at school.

The next school year came swiftly. The experience of meeting with the counsellors in my study for seven weeks, one evening a week, was an exciting and anxious time in the thesis process. The excitement came from the opportunity to research this question that had been with me for so long, and to meet with the counsellors over several weeks. At last, I could try out my ideas, put them into practice!

I was anxious about putting my ideas out through the research activities and having my colleagues participate in them and possibly criticize them or, worse, find them meaningless. I was opening up a part of myself that they did not see in our professional associations. At the same time I also knew that I was asking the counsellors to expose parts of their lives in our meetings. By being aware of my own vulnerability and by putting myself in the counsellors' shoes, I was able to create a comfortable atmosphere for our group and to talk about possible feelings of exposure that might come up in the experience. It would be through our willingness to enter into a dialogue with each other that we would learn about the connections between the personal and professional aspects of our lives.

The above reflection brings me to my stance as a researcher and how that developed throughout the thesis process. I was concerned about how to include myself in the research since I had made the decision to do so. My wanting to be an integral part of the thesis in an explicit way stemmed from a belief that the researcher brings her perceptions, ideas and beliefs to the work, and the truth of the work depends on including an acknowledgment of that fact. In earlier times, I had studied in the experimental psychology framework which used the objective scientific paradigm as its basis. I had had difficulty applying that paradigm to my notions of studying human behavior. I was not eager to engage in similar work.

That understood, however, expressing my experience was not an easy task for me. Although I had set up the methodology that would enable me to be an explicit part of my study as a researcher and as leader-participant in the study, when I came to the point of expressing myself I was engaged in another struggle. I wanted to write about my learnings throughout the thesis project and the ways I was changing and growing in that process. This required me to spend time in reflection so that I could connect to my experience at a deeper than mundane level.

The work of facing myself, of meeting the truth of my experience, and of recognizing myself was slow, hard work. I often felt as if I could name part of the experience but not all of it. The nuances were missing. At one point I took some of my writings about including myself to a close friend. She gave me the encouragement that I needed to continue my task by gently telling me that she thought I was still hiding part of myself and that I needed to probe deeper to find the words that I needed. In my discussion there is a section, "Including Myself" which is the result of my reflections and my encounter with my friend, and which expresses my learning process as I understood it at the time. Re-reading the section as I write this paragraph, I am struck by the continuity and progress in my learning over the years and by the opportunities that the thesis project gave me for my own learning.

The meaning that my thesis has for me, and I hope it has for others, was enriched by the inclusion of myself as researcher in it, as explicitly as I was able to be included at the time. It was an important part of my life process.

In the summer following the data collection part of the research project, I went to my cottage to begin working with the data. Using the method of constant comparison was both exciting and exacting work. I found that I worked best for uninterrupted stretches of time long enough for a tentative theme or idea to emerge. Then, after a rest period of some hours, going back to the data and the evolving patterns was often fruitful. Often this "rest" period was in the form of meditation and self-guided imagery work which enabled me to synthesize the ideas with which I was working. Evidence for themes became clearer and inter-connections became visible. Over several weeks, this process of intense work followed by rest resulted in themes that with some modifications became descriptors of the research experience. As I worked with these themes in terms of the counsellors' experience, I also understood them as reflecting my own knowing. The interconnections that emerged in my reflections, were an essential part of including myself in the thesis.

Writing the thesis took two years, and as the reader might expect by now, was not easy for me. I discovered that I was still enmeshed in my scientific training of being concise. My guide's careful reading of my writing, his sharing his insights and his gentle suggestions were invaluable. Rather than having to edit material that I had written, I definitely needed to become more discursive and fill in many details of the experience that I had omitted. The process was like preparing bread dough; adding flour and kneading until the dough became the right consistency. By the third draft I was finally writing in an appropriate style and the thesis was ready for my committee to read.

I was close to being completed and I was optimistic that I had written a work that would stand up with some modifications. Then one committee member was critical of the thesis suggesting revisions of such major proportions that I thought I would never complete my work. With support and encouragement from the other guides, I had a committee meeting and spoke to that committee member directly about my work. This proved to be a positive approach as he retracted much of the negative power in the criticism and the modifications that we agreed upon resulted in a more focussed and clearer work. In the end, the seemingly devastating event became the catalyst for improvement.

Throughout my journey, I was blessed with two guides who led the way. My supervisor guide created his part of the relationship with me in such a way that I felt respected and accepted in my process. I felt that he was truly a guide in suggesting possible ways to proceed and leaving the decisions to me. In concert with his carrying out his guiding activities with such integrity, I kept trying to work with the same integrity and do my very best work.

The journey was over but the learning continues to this day as I write this article. Through this writing I have journeyed back to the thesis-creating-time and, once again, I am reflecting on the self-knowledge I have gained. I love learning; even the hard, painful parts in which the deepest learning occurs. For me this "academic exercise" also provided important lessons for life.

Tips for Travellers

I have described some instances that may be helpful for the reader. In presenting my tips for travellers here, I have chosen some of those activities that had most meaning for me or with which I struggled the most.

- *Hold on to your idea; your idea will hold you.* If you have an idea about your study that engages you, spend some time working with it. Although you may not know where it will lead you, it probably has some important part to play in your journey.

- *Themes emerge from the data by staying with the data.* When you are analyzing the data and themes begin to emerge, keep in close touch with the raw data. Keep checking the themes with a variety of raw data to ensure that they are grounded in the truth of the experience. Go slow and steady. Using both analytical and synthetical methods can be helpful.

- *I take the thesis journey to go forward; to go forward, the thesis journey takes me.*
  This tip refers to sticking with the process, of taking one step after another in a forward direction towards completion of the thesis. By doing that the journey begins to take on an energy that in turn propels you forward. Keep going no matter how slowly or how many obstacles appear in the way.

- *Ask for what you need; need what you ask for.* In working with your guides, be clear and direct about what you need. Before doing that, however, reflect on the matter, to see if you really need their help or if what you need to do is work some more to find the answer within yourself. When you do this then the meetings with your guides will tend to be focussed and effective.

- *In an outward search, look inward.* Take the opportunity to learn about yourself by "beginning with your-self" (Hunt, 1987) as you take the thesis journey. The knowledge revealed in your work will be grounded in the focal experience researched as well as your own experience as researcher, thus containing more ele-ments of the truth of the experience.

- *I open to serendipity; serendipity opens to me.* By being open to chance events that come to you during your journey you may discover an untrodden path that will take you to significant learnings. This hap-pening can greatly enrich your work.

If I Were a Guide. . .

I would enter into a partnership with the traveller in which we mutually agree upon the nature and form of our com-mitments to each other. My first and ongoing task would be to develop and maintain a relationship that was en-hancing to the traveller achieving her goal. It would be important to me to make explicit the opportunity to check in with each other periodically regarding the quality of that relationship and to talk about any areas of concern.

Sharing would be an important aspect of this partner-ship. I would seek ways to share my ideas, insights and feelings when asked by the traveller or by offering them when I thought appropriate. Through thoughtful reading and commentary of work in progress, I would hope to facilitate the traveller's writing process. I would encourage the traveller to be reflective, to have patience with the hard parts and to keep moving forward.

I would really listen to what the traveller was trying to tell me. To receive the traveller in this way, I think I could help her or him find the answers to questions. By re-phrasing what I heard, by asking a variety of types of questions (i.e., open ended, focal) I would hope to help the traveller sharpen her analytical and synthetical thinking abilities.

In terms of time and setting practicalities, I would en-courage the traveller to set realistic goals and to ensure that there was a place to work undistracted for significant periods of time.

In my role, I would be available for consultations at agreed upon times. My commitment to the partnership between us would be a crucial and positive force in the progress of the work.

Guides and travellers are essential partners in any successful journey in which one person is exploring new territory. The quality of the traveller's experience in many
significant aspects such as load to carry, time to take,
maps to follow and so forth will be greatly enhanced by a
good guide. In turn, I expect that the guide's experience is
also enriched in the relationship that is formed with the
traveller in that old territory, and may reveal surprises
and nuances of meaning as uncovered through the new
eyes of the traveller. For each, then, the journey is a new
venture full of the promise of life.

Finding A Voice and Giving Voice to Teachers

Mary Beattie

Thesis Title:

The Making of Relations: A Narrative Study of the Construction and Reconstruction of a Teacher's Personal Practical Knowledge

Unpublished doctoral thesis,
University of Toronto, 1990.

Touchstone

For as long as I can remember,
I have noticed sounds.
The crow's harsh caw, the soft
squelch of boggy ground
And the songs inside stones.
They became the soundscapes of a mind,
Shaped by stories and by stone.
Grey wind-swept limestone,
In circles rippling back in time,
Forming ancient texts that have marked
*   my soul.*

"Don't go near those bogs" they said,
"Those bottomless holes will suck you down
And you'll never be heard of again."
I skirt the soft and springy moss,
The small brown pools and ferny ways.

Searching for stone-full voice and sound
And heard as if for the first time now,
Echoing the music of the marrow-bone.

(Beattie, *Touchstone*, November, 1990)

The process of engaging in the thesis journey was a process of re-discovering my own inner voice and of collaborat-
ing with Anne (the teacher/participant in my study) to
raise our voices together to talk about the qualities of
change, growth and professional development from the
teacher's perspective. Teaching, learning, relationships,
stories and music are central to who I am as a person and
in order to write a thesis that would be meaningful and
satisfying for me, I had to connect the work I would do in
an academic environment to my inner self and to the
things that have value and importance for me. I chose as
my teachers those who encouraged me to go inwards, to
explore my inner self and to find my own authentic voice
and ways of knowing. It was with the help of these teachers that I came to see the research and the writing as
opportunities for gaining increased self-knowledge on the
part of the researcher and participant, and for engaging in
collaborative experiences which would enrich both of our
lives as we generated new knowledge about professional
development and educational change.

Through the research and the writing, I learned that
growth and professional renewal for teachers requires the
continual making and remaking of a new unity of the self
as the teacher/learner becomes increasingly more responsive to external voices and to harmonize them with the
internal voice. The return wave of consequences from this
kind of research and these understandings had a significant impact on my own professional life. I became increasingly aware of the need to improve my own capacities as a
teacher of future teachers and to create better learning
situations for my pre-service students within which they
would be encouraged to develop their own voices, and to
experience for themselves the kind of teaching I hoped they
would act out in their own classrooms. I became increasingly aware that I needed to help them to increase their
abilities to respond to the voices of others and to create
classrooms of their own where the curriculum is co-cre-
ated and where voices are joined in the music of collaborative learning and growth.

The field-based part of my study and my work with Anne
in her classroom took place over a two-year period. I wrote
a lot of field notes, letters, accounts and summaries of our
work together, and I kept a record of my ongoing thoughts,
questions, dilemmas and tentative understandings in a

thesis journal throughout. Two years after my thesis oral, I finally threw out all this material (except for the thesis journal) and it filled six, big, black garbage bags. I knew that I had enough data for about four theses but as I watched the garbage truck take the bags away, I had no regrets....one thesis is enough....there is other writing waiting to be done, other voices waiting to be heard and other stories waiting to be told.

Writing the Music of Classroom Life

From start to finish, the research and the writing of the thesis took five years and each phase presented me with a highly significant set of learning experiences. I loved the intensity of these experiences and the way they added to the quality of my life. I loved the feeling of breaking through the boundaries of my understandings and the glimpses of unexplored territory which continually came into view. It was, however, the actual writing itself which gave me the most joy. I have countless memories of late nights and early mornings sitting at my computer, warm breezes blowing in from the garden and words and phrases coming together on the screen in front of me. I have memories of blocks, failed experiments and a stiff, sore back and legs too but, somehow, it is the times when it all came together and I felt the joy of creation that I remember best. I saw the writing as an opportunity to bring together my interests in teaching, in learning, in literature and in music; a unique opportunity to describe the world as I know it. I wanted to see how different literary forms could be used to make the music of classroom life, to show the qualities and complexities of teacher learning and growth, of collaborative professional relationships and of the lived experiences of professional development and change. My hope was that my words would resonate for other teachers, teacher educators and researchers and that they would recognize them as expressing true sounding aspects of their own experience. On behalf of all teachers, I hoped that I would, in Seamus Heaney's words:

> ....fill the air with signatures on (our) own frequency
> Echo soundings, searches, probes, allurements,
> elver-gleams in the dark of the whole sea.

The thesis was written in three parts which are three interconnecting stories. I began with my own story of teaching and learning and followed with Anne's story of change, growth and professional development, and our story of collaboration and interaction. All three stories are stories of making new unities and of, in T.S. Eliot's words,

> *arriv(ing) where we started,*
> *And know(ing) the place for the first time."*

Individually and collaboratively, we learned to write the stories of ourselves in new ways, as the research, the collaborative reflection and the writing opened up new possibilities, showed the potential for the making of new relations and offered the opportunity to make a new form that was personally and professionally transforming. Old stories of the self were replaced by new, richer, more significant stories which fit the current situations and the futures we foresaw. As Anne said at the end "It is a question of seeing things in different ways.... They are the same things, but I can now see them in new ways."

The experience of finding a voice, of using it to enable others to do likewise, and of making significant music together, is one that irreversibly changes the quality and direction of one's life. It is joyful, energizing, empowering and aesthetically pleasing to create meanings and to tell stories through which others feel invited and encouraged to raise questions about their own practices and ways of knowing, to make their own meanings and to tell their own stories. These experiences were profound aesthetic achievements for me and they created a need to recreate the circumstances through which the joy and delight that the process of creation and music making makes possible, could be felt again. As a teacher, I'm still actively engaged with the question of what it means to create learning environments where learners find their own voices and become increasingly more adept at the articulation of beliefs, values, images and understandings, where they inquire into the underlying structures of their own knowing, come to hear new possibilities through their interactions with others and re-create a new and more significant unity for the self. As a writer, I'm drawn to the reconciliation of content and form through the act of creating patterns with words, patterns that resonate for a reader and that are recognized as expressing true sounding, authentic aspects of the reader's internal feelings. I'm still drawn to the telling of stories, stories within which people can live vicariously, can imagine new possibilities other than the ones they know and through which they are empowered to tell and retell the stories of their own lives. I think I'll always be drawn to what I have come to understand as the expression of inner realities through words, to the documentation of my own "inner music," to describing the world as I know it as a person who is also a professional teacher.

The first chapter in my thesis started with an excerpt from T.S. Eliot's poem "Four Quartets";

> *We shall not cease from exploration*
> *And the end of all our exploring*
> *Will be to arrive where we started*
> *And know the place for the first time.*

These words perfectly expressed my inner intentions and hopes for the thesis journey, my felt need to journey backwards in order to move forwards and to acknowledge that all my beginnings have held within them the seeds of their own endings, which in themselves have held the seeds of new beginnings. The final chapter of the thesis began with my own poem, "Touchstone", (which I used to begin this chapter) and whose purpose it was to express the qualities of the thesis journey by looking back over it and looking forward to the new end approaching and the new beginnings being born. As I said there, my search for a true, authentic voice which would express the "inner music" of self and others, had been a search for a "stone-full voice and sound." The writing was the instrument through which this voice could "Echo the music of the marrowbone" and play this "inner music" aloud, hopeful of setting up a corresponding resonance in the reader by expressing true sounding aspects of her experience and by giving external voice to something essential, something felt internally and previously unarticulated.

Tuning In to the Inner Music

There is an old Irish proverb that says: "Go to Rome, little profit. The God you seek lives at home." It is good advice for anyone setting out on this marvellous but unpredictable thesis journey. It advises the traveller to begin by exploring the mysteries and the influences of his or her own understandings and to tune in to the sounds of one's own inner music. It seems to say that the answers to our most significant questions lie within us and that the search for meaning and fulfilment will only be thwarted if it begins outside of ourselves. The wise traveller chooses a teacher-guide who will encourage and support the search for this authentic voice and will value the gifts which each traveller brings to the journey. This traveller knows that the influence of such a teacher will be a guiding light through the joyful and the difficult times, a light that will illuminate possibilities not immediately visible to the first-time traveller. Having such a travelling companion, this traveller takes a long, close look at the purpose and de-sired experiences of the proposed journey and at the ways in which the travelling and the achievement of the destina-tion is expected to enrich and enhance the lives of all those involved. The journey that will transform can then be embarked upon; it will have its ebb and its flow and its steep hills and lush, green valleys, before the final destina-tion is reached. It will also have its ever constant vision of enriched and transformed lives at journey's end; lives that will go journeying again, sometimes as travellers on further explorations of their own and sometimes as guides with new and inexperienced travellers.

Epilogue

On Wednesday, September 22, 1993, the Publishing Board at Teachers College Press approved the acceptance of the manuscript of my thesis for publication as a book. This message was waiting for me on my answering machine when I returned home at 9.30 p.m. that evening. I listened to the message over and over again, revelling in the sweet music of the words and the sheer joy of what they meant to me. They told me that sometimes dreams do come true.

The Tao of Writing a Thesis

Elizabeth J. Burge

Thesis Title

**Students' Perceptions of Learning in
Computer Conferencing:
A Qualitative Analysis**

Unpublished doctoral thesis, University of Toronto, 1993.

This chapter is the result of several actual exchanges of
FAXES (facsimile transmissions) between a Finnish friend
and colleague, Eila Öhrmark, and myself. Our letters have
been edited because each of us digressed somewhat as we
explored some topics. My thesis topic focused on students'
perceptions of learning as they worked through a graduate
course that was run almost entirely in a computer conference mode. I wanted to find out how they thought they
learned, what features of the mode most influenced their
learning, and how their strategies compared with a set
found in cognitive psychology. A qualitative approach was
used — in-depth interviewing with transcript coding and
analysis using grounded theory methods.

The Letters

Dear E,

We were talking recently about your "doing" a doctoral thesis and I found myself reflecting about mine. So
here are a few of those reflections, sent to encourage you to
proceed.

How do I start? Let me take an eagle's eye view of the
terrain. The details (the worm's eye view) are contained in

the books about writing a thesis. The big issues for me were time and the conditions for being creative.

Time availability was an issue because I worked full-time (often over-time, like you do) and it was all too easy to allow other writing, research or administrative tasks to deflect my attention and deplete my thesis time. Finally, I realized, and not without some pushing from my supervisor, that I would have to push everything else aside, practice saying "no" to requests, and just hunker down for the final months of high energy periods of writing and editing. That strategy worked, and indeed had worked at two earlier stages — the data gathering and the data analysis — but I'd almost forgotten the benefits of such energy bursts. Time — to focus on the task, to daydream, to think, to re-think, to regain energy — was definitely a precious commodity for me. I had to "buy" it from vacation time or exchange it from overtime work (or, as Dorothy MacKeracher calls it, over-work time). I experienced time also in a qualitative sense — as periods of high and low will-power, and periods of high and low creativity.

In terms of will-power, I went through very definite periods of feeling guilty when I suffered from the condition that Ogden Nash satirized so well — velleity:

> it means low degree of volition not
> prompting to action,
> and I always knew I had something holding me-
> back but I didn't know what,
> And it's quite a relief to know it isn't a conspiracy,
> it's only velleity
> I've got....

At first I castigated myself greatly for this state of mind and feeling. Words such as "lazy," "unfocused," and "incompetent" circled around in my head like a repetitive audio tape. I forced myself to work sometimes when I had no cognitive energy, and ended up feeling even worse! In *The Tao of Pooh* is a wonderful description of the net result:

> Try doing something with a tense mind. The
> surest way to become Tense, Awkward and Con-
> fused is to develop a mind that tries too hard—
> one that thinks too much (Hoft, 1982, p. 77).

I learned that my thinking, feeling and doing activities had their own ebbs and flows of energy, and that I was being foolish and disrespectful if I tried to push through the time periods that appeared to be unproductive. In reality my mind was just cooking away nicely but it wasn't ready to have its "cake" pulled from the oven. Victoria Nelson has a neat metaphor:

> We know already that "laziness" and "stalling" are the buzzwords of an autocratic, punishing consciousness. That consciousness is unaware that anything is happening because the unconscious is shielding its sprouting seeds from the prematurely judgemental ego. Consciousness will not be allowed in the garden until the plants are tall enough and tough enough to withstand its hobnailed boots. Then, and only then, will it be granted entry (Nelson, 1993, p. 164).

I learned that I needed a compassionate kind of self-discipline; one that kept me on task when the garden began to sprout new growth, but one that also allowed me to let go when the soil looked barren.

In terms of creativity and periods of time, several things happened. I developed a new respect for my thinking process, even as I interviewed to collect my data. Because I feared missing anything important and time was short, I adopted a state of almost aggressive attentiveness to what was being said, and sometimes too quickly jumped into the conversation to clarify what I was hearing. I didn't treat time in the interview as a harmonious, creative "white space" where I could adopt states of relaxed attentiveness and trust that the interviewee — if she/he also has enough "white space," or silence — would use that time to think, reflect or speculate, and so give potentially richer data.

Elspeth Huxley's book, *The Flame Trees of Thika,* has a few relevant lines about connectedness and attentiveness that made sense to me only after several interviews had occurred and I had thought about how one finds information in the world:

> If you sit quite still and pretend not to be looking, all the little facts will come and peck round your feet, situations will venture forth from thickets, and intentions will creep out and sun themselves on a stone. (Huxley, 1959, p. 248).

I also experienced very definite periods of creative writing when everything seemed to flow together without obstruction. For example, ideas seemed to come together when I trusted myself enough to write-in-order-to-think, rather than think-in-order-to-write. Sometimes, only as I put pen to paper, did I see what I knew. And with what feelings of delight! A side benefit to this kind of writing was the making of room in my crowded head for new ideas to begin floating around and growing. It was as if I had to "let go," or clean out some plants (and weeds) before the next round of gardening.

But in between those periods of creativity? Horrors!! As one Canadian writer described it:

> Between those epiphanic moments of joy are days and days of miles and miles straining against a prairie headwind" (Lennie, 1993).

When I strained against the winds of unreadiness or confusion, I got myself into trouble. I felt blocked. I produced words on the paper that were dense, or helped no one understand anything. As Truman Capote described it, "that's not writing, that's typing!"

Oops! By now I thought the letter would be listing more academic issues of thesis production, but instead my memory has been stuck fast in the more practical, operational matters.

Looking forward to your reactions!

Sincerely,

L

* * * *

Dear L,

Your letter made me stop and think . . . Here are some scattered comments.

Why not, as a title for your chapter, the "Tao of writing a thesis"? . . .
I (think I) "understand" the Taoist "The Way Things Work" and am ready to agree it would suffice as such as an orientation. I remember once asking somebody what she considered the five most important things in "doing" a doctoral thesis. She answered: "Patience, patience, patience, patience and patience. . . "

I very much agree with your eagle's eye view and the worm's approach as well as your analysis of time. I also feel a sting in my consciousness, because I realize there

will be many an encounter with both velleity and "an auto-
cratic, punishing consciousness" on my way towards the
goal. Are you saying one SHOULD not start writing a
thesis unless it is the thing you want to sacrifice everything else for?

What advice do you give to somebody who cannot quit
work or "established" duties, cannot put their families,
ailing parents and other dependents into the fridge for
months: Are they doomed?

I close for now, agreeing that nothing succeeds when
done with "a tense mind" and a "punishing consciousness," knowing that "travelling is better than arriving" and
therefore asking you: How do I learn to love my thesis? . . .

Sincerely,

E

* * * *

Dear E,

Yes, indeed, why not "The Tao of Writing a Thesis" as a
title? The wisdom of Tao stresses both the underlying
harmony in how things operate, our connectedness with
that harmony, and our futility in resisting the natural
flows of events in the universe.

I would not dare confront the question of loving that you
pose, but let's deal with your feelings of doom and sacrifice. Sacrifice shouldn't be too drastic. Negotiate with
yourself and with key "others" in your life some time and
effort boundaries. No-one, not even competent you, can
add on a thesis to your existing life-load, so some things
have to give — perhaps smaller amounts of time spent with
family, or reduced contact with friends. I found that I
needed time off to restore my psychic energies, but that I
became very choosy regarding with whom I spent recrea-
tional time: they had to be understanding if I appeared
tired or vague, and they also had to be capable of some
"tough love" when my self-confidence wavered. It's the
quality of your nurture, not its quantity, that counts.

Don't feel "doomed." Feel determined. How? First,
establish an overall time boundary for the whole project.
Second, negotiate with your supervisor a reasonable thesis
length. My supervisor was clear: he did not want a huge
"tome," and that anyway I should have the skills to write
succinctly.

Third, choose a topic that you "own." Even if you do not

learn to love your thesis with a passion, it is much easier to control the occasional panic attack and maintain your self-esteem and identity if your choice of topic is one of high personal interest.   Margaret Wall's master's thesis investigation of women's experiences of graduate study at the University of New Brunswick found that the Self was a crucial focus for thesis writers:

> The thesis created an opportunity to integrate the inner and outer experiences of self and to resolve some of the feelings of conflict the women experienced during their coursework and other program activities. For most participants, the thesis experience helped define self as competent, as a person, and within their discipline. For those who completed the process, the thesis also provided each woman with an opportunity to increase the personal relevance of her program of study, to increase her feelings of connections between self and ideas and self and others in her graduate program (Wall, 1992, p. 82).

Fourth, do all you can to feel in control. I felt competent when I felt in control. Those times were finalizing the research question (I kept it to a manageable scope), gathering the data (I felt the excitement and security in the sheer quantity of data), and finishing chunks of writing (I could see what I knew). But during other stages, I felt quite the opposite! and often allowed feelings of loss of control, self-doubts, and apparent lack of direction to create some "cold mists" of indecision or apprehension. Those stages were transcribing the interviews (a veritable flood of data!), beginning the data analysis (will it be sophisticated enough?) and deciding what to exclude from the final written version (everything feels essential!). In Margot Ely's excellent book, there's a great statement about this reality of self-responsibility:

> [We] have found that often the first analyses create a place where reality hits, where doubts, fears, and avoidances begin...When the researcher gets right to it, it is an awesome, even frightening responsibility to bow to the fact that 'self-as-instrument' inevitably means one must create ongoing meaning out of the evolving and

evolved data, since raw data alone have little
value (Ely,1991, p. 86).

Fifth, liberate yourself from any "voices" that say you must
always turn in chapter drafts of 120% quality. I found that
sometimes I kept my momentum and concentration going
if I gave my supervisor a draft that was 90%, on the understanding that I wanted some guidance before finishing the
10%. Consistent perfection is a deadly, delusionary standard!

I do not agree with your friend's list of the five most
important things in "doing" a doctoral thesis, i.e., patience,
because that quality does not fit well with my learnings
about maintaining a pro-active stance. Some days, what
propelled my body and my mind was impatience! My five
key things are Boundaries (of time on and scope of thesis),
Balance (between action and reflection, between thesis and
life loads), Relevance (of the topic), Nutrition (I underesti-
mated this one), and an Editor (essential for dispassionate
assessments of clarity and sheer reader interest, and for
catching errors you cannot see).

That's all for now,

L

* * * *

Dear L,

It would, indeed, be nice to go rambling into the garden
of philosophy, your last letter was so inspiring. It would be
extremely interesting to enlarge on M. Wall's passage about
the importance of the Self. The Self is not only a crucial
focus for thesis writers. Isn't it for all conscious existence?
How can we integrate "inner or outer experiences" or anything without knowing "who/what we are?"

But how about the structuring of the substance of the
thesis? Is there a certain preferred structure for the arrangement of the material? Does it depend somehow on
the chosen approach? I mean whether one chooses one's
thesis to be descriptive, analytical, or "interpretative?"

Will you say something about the style and language?
The Swedish poet Gustaf Fröding said "Det klart tänkta,
är det klart sagda" : "what is clearly thought, is clearly
said, or what is not clearly thought cannot be clearly said."
The enormous expressiveness of poetry lies in its brevity.

You spoke too about succinctness. Is the borderline

between (poetic) brevity and ambiguity clear enough? In [some] parts of the world it seems that length and pompous/jargon language is often thought/hoped to be signs of quality in scientific work.

Somebody once said "Science describes reality, art creates reality." Is this to be taken as a measuring stick? . . I claim that Tao applies to science and thesis writing too. And therefore it should allow a much wider choice of structure and styles than is customary. . .

On this meeting ground I think I could easily learn to love my thesis. . .

Sincerely,
E

* * * *

Dear E,

You raise complex issues! First, let me make one personal link between the Self and style.

It took me a while to become accustomed to using "I" and "me" in my writing. Initially it took some courage because it meant, in effect, publicizing my own values and standing up for my beliefs and judgements; no hiding behind personal anonymity or displays of academic knowledge. I found also that this approach needs great clarity of expression.

Here's where I would qualify your term brevity. Brevity in writing style is a noble and necessary criterion, but it demands the right quality of words. Images and metaphors, as well as prosaic (literal?) words, have to adequately describe the richness of data and the interpretations of that data.

Regarding your concern about pompous language: Yes!! Displays of academic "feathers" have limited uses, and should be banned altogether if they leave any reader feeling confused or overwhelmed. Let's hope that it's only insecure thesis students who feel the need to obfuscate.

You ask if there is a meeting ground between art and science: it's a good question that needs a better response than I can give here. I think it was Gandhi who said "It is precisely because they wear the warmth and color of the senses that the arts are the most educative of all forces." I like that! So the struggle in my thesis was to render some of the warmth and color of real humans without losing the academic rigor for a qualitative study. There is now much literature on this issue of rigor. For me, a thesis and a work of art always have to observe the relevant canons of design, of execution/method, and expression of the artist's/writer's final interpretation of reality as they must describe it. But let me think some more, and recommend that you look at theses using the naturalistic paradigm.

Let me close with several comments about the relationship with your supervisor. One senior professor at OISE expressed the thesis supervisor-student relationship as an "academic courtship." I guess if a student is impressionable, or has little experience in completing lengthy conceptual and writing tasks, the courtship activities of developing "favor" and pleasing someone may be perceived as relevant. And, of course, a student has very definite limits of power within the academic institution. But I took the stance that if I balanced being pro-active (e.g., saying what I wanted to do, before negotiating from there) and being responsive to my supervisor's reactions (he had directed more theses than I even knew about), then my chances of completing the thesis would be enhanced. So, E, choose your supervisor with great care. Choose one who is not only experienced, but who is empathetic to the stresses upon part-time doctoral students, and who will not be shocked or offended if you talk plainly about your boundaries of time and thesis length. A doctoral thesis is not your Life's Work, but it is a biggish project. It can be enjoyed — for its engagement of your Self, as well as your production of new knowledge. David Sternberg's book (1981) has some marvellously pragmatic and unabashedly honest comments about how to survive the whole thesis; it's worth a read.

Bon Voyage, and keep in touch.
Sincerely,
L

I Remember. . . Critical Incidents of the Thesis Journey

Ardra L. Cole

Thesis Title

**Teachers' Spontaneous Adaptations:
A Mutual Interpretation**

Unpublished doctoral thesis, University of Toronto, 1987.

I remember a lot about my thesis journey. How could I forget? It was the single most personally meaningful and important experience (event) of my adult life. It was transformative, an epiphany. Travelling that journey privileged me for many subsequent opportunities, among them being a guide to less experienced travellers. In recent years I have had the privilege of working with and supervising doctoral students at various points along *their* thesis journey. As I engage formally and informally with these new travellers — sometimes following, sometimes leading, and other times walking alongside — I am frequently flashed back to my own experience as a traveller. I remember the journey as a challenging, exhilarating, and richly rewarding experience yet one which was at times arduous, seemingly endless, and very lonely. My travelling experience and knowledge of the terrain from the perspective of a student-traveller now guide me as I try to guide others.

In this account I remember "critical incidents" of my own thesis journey, times and events of particular significance to me when I was a traveller, and which have retained their significance in my work as a guide. My recollections each begin with an emotive response mainly because when I think back to my thesis work, what I remember first is how I felt at certain times and places. Reflecting further on those incidents I uncover the lessons learned along the way.

I remember. . . the innumerable bouts of self-doubt and anxiety that seemed to block my path from the outset to the end of the journey. I also remember moments of self-confidence when I was inspired and moved forward. One moment in particular stands out when I knew that my mother was right, there *was* "no such word as can't."   I *could* do it — write a thesis, that is.

Although it is commonly understood that writing a thesis is part of doctoral work, I wonder how many people know at the outset what a thesis is or involves. I did not. In an effort to understand the nature and extent of the task I was undertaking I spent hours in the library reading examples of recently completed theses in my area of interest (teaching and teacher development). I figured that seeing some finished products would help me find some direction. I made a mistake by first selecting exemplary pieces of work that I had often heard about or seen cited or that had been recommended to me by professors. I became overwhelmed, convinced that I was not up to the challenge. At that point I did not have the wisdom of hindsight to realize that the works I was reading shone from hours of polishing and that I had not see them in their unrefined forms; nor did I have the self-confidence to believe that I had what it took to produce a work of this substance and quality.

And then, quite by accident, I picked up another thesis, also relevant to my area of study but one that I had not heard about. Suddenly the task seemed less daunting. Perhaps it was because this thesis was written in a style that was accessible, more understandable to me at the time, or perhaps it was because overall, even according to my naive standards, it was less than exemplary. For whatever reason, for the first time, I could actually see myself as a thesis writer. I became very aware of a newfound confidence in myself and I moved ahead.

I remember. . . the feeling of liberation that came with having my thesis proposal approved, and how that affirmation helped me to trust in myself and my abilities. I had spent months engaged in the inexplicably difficult processes of finding a topic, focusing, conducting a preliminary study, and then developing a proposal to carry out the "real" study. My thesis proposal was substantial in quantity. I used it as a vehicle to work through ideas and develop a plan. I also wanted to ensure the approval of my thesis committee members so I labored over every detail — what I thought was important *to them*. What was most important to me at that time was getting *their* approval so that I could do *my* study. And I did.

The climax of the committee meeting at which I presented my proposal came when the approval form was passed and signed, without hesitation, by all members. That moment of approval was a liberating experience. I interpreted the consent of my committee members as an expression of confidence in me and my potential to carry out the work I proposed. That affirmation inspired me with the self-confidence I needed to push on. It was a turning point in my journey. It was the beginning of an ever-strengthening belief in and trust of *my* judgements, *my* intuitions, and *my* voice. From then on, what I did and what I wrote was *for me*.

I remember. . . worrying throughout the early stages of my field work about whether I would be able to gather enough information to enable me to write a thesis on my topic, and whether the information I was gathering was of any use. Everything I had read about conducting qualitative research insisted that researchers come to "know" when they have enough information and, even in spite of this, they usually end up with far more information than they can realistically use. I felt certain, in the early part of my work, that I was to be an exception to these rules. But then as I watched my pile of data (field notes, interview transcripts, journal entries, preliminary analyses) daily grow, I began to appreciate both the quantity and the quality of the information I was gathering. I realized that what was described in the qualitative methods books was true. The information was plentiful and rich, and I did come to know when it was time to stop. Once again, I realized the importance of trusting my judgement and intuition.

I remember. . . the frenetic pace I kept throughout the information gathering phase of my work in particular. Because I had agreed to provide the teachers in my study a transcript of each weekly interview and a summary of the field notes of my weekly visits to their classroom before we met each time, it seemed like I was always racing against the clock. Hour after hour of seemingly endless transcribing, and poring over field notes to extract essential elements of my observations and impressions paid off in the long run though. This commitment to the teachers in my study kept me on track and gave me deadlines to meet which, in retrospect, was significant in accelerating me toward completion.

I remember. . . the thrill I experienced when analysing the data I had been gathering for several months. I remember comparing the process of data analysis to the experience of receiving a gift — one carefully nestled in layer upon layer of delicate wrapping. When I returned to research methods texts for guidance I was reminded by one author that analysis of qualitative data is the most creative part of research and also the hardest to describe — perhaps because it is such a creative process. I wanted to preserve the integrity of the information I had gathered, and to discover, not impose, meaning, so the more prescriptive and traditional methods for data interpretation were inadequate for my purposes. I was left, therefore, to try to understand the meaning of interpretation and analysis, and believe those who insisted that the data would eventually begin to "make sense," "feel right," and that themes and ideas would "flow" from it. All of this was initially very intimidating; however, once I decided to start gingerly removing the wrapping I experienced almost immediate gratification and relief. After immersing myself in the data it *really did* talk. The interpretation process *really was* an ongoing conversation. Themes *did* flow. Patterns *did* emerge. And, eventually it *did* make sense and feel right. Once again, I learned to trust not only myself and my judgements but also the data and the interpretation process.

I remember. . . that wonderful moment of revelation — the "aha" experience — when, suddenly and inexplicably, "it" all came together and made sense, and I could see, for the first time, exactly how the thesis needed to be written and what needed to be said. The weeks and months of brooding, musing, and often fretting over the data came to a close one evening at a time I least expected.

A local recreation park regularly hosted open air concerts for extremely low prices. They, and second-run films, were about the only cultural indulgences I could afford. This night Branford Marsalis was performing. I arrived early for a good seat, the ever-present transcripts in hand (no sense wasting time). I used the time before the concert to participate in the seemingly endless ritual of reading interview transcripts, hoping for and willing *something* to happen. After all, "they" said it would, eventually. Two hours into the concert, transcripts and overt thoughts of my work safely tucked away, "Eureka!" Suddenly and for no explicable reason I understood what the data was telling me and how to respond. Although I had trouble containing my excitement, I managed to refrain from running naked through the streets, or even from sharing my discovery with my neighbour who I am certain would have thought me quite daft.

I remember. . . the smiles and nods, and the glazed looks of friends and family kind enough to ask, "So, how's your research/work/school going (or coming)?" It took me a very long time to realize that that question was not to be taken too literally; it was akin to "Hello, how are you?" I also realized that what they really meant was "When will you be finished?" or "You're not finished yet!"

Writing a thesis is a very lonely and all-consuming process and no one outside the academic community understands, or really even cares to know, exactly what you are doing and why. Both the pleasures and the pains of the journey can really only be felt in all their intensity by the traveller. It is difficult, if not impossible, for someone unfamiliar with the thesis process, to understand it. It is unfair to expect otherwise.

I remember. . . moving to the rhythm the thesis set for me, revelling in the focused intensity of the task, and finding — to use Virginia Woolf's (1928) phrase both literally and metaphorically — "a room of my own." Seeing Toronto's Bloor Street (where the university is located) at 3:00 a.m. became a commonplace occurrence. It was at this time that I regularly emerged from "my cloistered space away from the common sitting room" where I experienced in Gail Griffin's (1992) words, "the joy of being in a place where the significance of one's work is assumed and takes priority over all else" (p. 230). There, I discovered and listened to my inner rhythm and found a way of maintaining my commitment to the task.

I remember. . . the pain of hardships endured and the constant challenge to, or test of, my strength and commitment. Personal costs and sacrifices — material, relational, and otherwise — pressures associated with desperate financial straits, and family traumas of serious illness, death, and marital separation were at times seemingly insurmountable mountains to be crossed. Completing the thesis journey requires, perhaps more than anything else, stubborn determination and persistence. As someone once said, "Nothing takes the place of persistence."

I remember. . . the physical and psychological nourishment I grew to depend on through the long walks that became such an important part of "my process." During the five to ten miles I covered every day, either en route to and from the university or on less purposeful hikes, I thought through ideas, maintained contact with the world around me, re-energized my tired mind and body, and dreamed of being finished. I envisaged the final product in various ways at different times. I envisaged what the analysis would look like and how the "cases" would be presented. I even envisaged the completed thesis on the library shelf bound in blue leatherette with gold lettering. I fantasized about life after thesis when I could read whatever I wanted and when I might make up for some lost time and experiences. I imagined myself employed as an academic, actually being paid to read, think, research, and write. Taking the time each day to visualize the light at the end of the tunnel and maintaining a certain level of physical fitness helped me to move forward.

I remember. . . the mixture of joy and disbelief I invariably experienced whenever my supervisor (ever sensitive to the sense of urgency connected with writing a thesis and remarkably adept at reading and responding quickly to drafts) called to tell me that my work was "in good shape." Not that I needed the extrinsic reinforcement, I assured myself, but for some reason I worked faster and more confidently after those phone calls or meetings. I worked out what I thought was a reasonable timeline for the completion of the thesis, and we agreed that I would submit a draft of each chapter when it was completed and he would respond as soon as possible. A combination of my compulsion to stick to deadlines, my supervisor's support and encouragement of my work, and our mutual respect for our working relationship was a constant source of inspiration.

I remember. . . the thrill and gratification of accomplishment and near completion. I remember standing at the printer late one night (or, more accurately, early one morning) waiting with nervous delight and quiet anticipation for the safe delivery of the final draft of my thesis, smiling proudly as each page presented itself intact, and periodically giving the growing bundle an affectionate and approving pat. I remember carrying it carefully, oh so carefully, to my office and closing the door on it for the night, quietly so as not to stir the pages — at least until later in the day.

I remember. . . the anxiety that permeated my body and mind, and the boundless, nervous energy that I could not contain on the day before my final oral examination. I felt like my future was in someone else's hands. Although all signs pointed to a successful examination I was reluctant to be overly confident. I remember thinking, "Tomorrow I will (hopefully) realize my high-priced dream. And then what? What about the day after? Will those books I have been saving to read still have an appeal? Will I know what to do in my life-after-thesis? Will any (even one) of my numerous job applications pay off? Back to tomorrow, will I remember what my thesis was about? Will I be able to answer the questions of my examining committee?"

My supervisor telephoned me the night before the defense to give me yet another vote of confidence and some final words of advice to get a good night's sleep and to remind myself that *I* was the expert on my topic. Easy for him to say!

I remember. . . planning a party for the evening of my defense. What else was there to do in the time between the final submission to the examining committee and the day of the oral examination? Besides, I figured that whatever the outcome I would need the party. Really though, the party was to be a celebration of many things: of my accomplishment, of the end of the long and arduous journey, and of friendship and support. And it was. Not only was it important for me to recognize what I had done but, more important, to recognize those who had accompanied me along the way with their encouragement, patience, and support. Although the thesis journey is a solitary one, its completion is a significant event to the sideline supporters as well. It was important for me to give something back to those who had given so much so that I could realize my dream. Celebrating the end of the journey was important for all of us.

And, *I remember*. . . that moment when I was called

back into the examination room and heard, "Congratulations, Dr. Cole."

The things I remember of my travelling experience I remind myself of as a guide:

- A thesis is completed through persistence and determination.
- Completing a thesis is a lonely process characterized by highs and lows. Embrace and celebrate the joys and rest assured that frustrations eventually will dissipate and points of dissonance will find resolution.
- The thesis process is pervaded by uncertainty and self-doubt. Writing a thesis is as much about personal growth and developing confidence and trust in yourself as it is about anything else.
- Setting and working to deadlines helps to move things along.
- A supportive supervisor who is sincerely interested in facilitating the completion of your thesis is your greatest ally.
- Revel in the process.
- Envisage and celebrate the end of the journey.

I Did It My Way!

Catherine Comuzzi

Thesis Title:

Trying to Catch the Wind: Subtle and Covert Discrimination Against Professional Women in the Workplace

Unpublished doctoral thesis, University of Toronto, 1992.

Introduction

At the party to celebrate the successful completion of my doctoral thesis, my close friend presented me with a symbol of her conceptualization of my research journey — a doll of myself, dressed in disheveled graduation gown, diploma in hand, hair sticking startlingly straight up tied with string, and proudly flaunting a banner across her chest which read: " I did it my way!" Indeed, "doing it my way" had involved charting my own unique path through thorny patches of high tension and release in what had been a major personal and scholarly challenge.   From the distinct advantage of hindsight, I came to see how the process of facing and resolving the many critical dialectical moments in the thesis struggle were inevitable and un-avoidable. For me, confronting the moments of "crisis" that arose in the process of writing my doctoral thesis afforded me substantial opportunities for personal and professional growth in three distinct ways: I experienced the gradual evolution of my ability to face and to interact with these moments, in order to release a new direction, a new decision, a new understanding; I developed my capacity to hold emotional and intellectual chaos until a deeper sense of order emerged; and I cultivated my keenness for sensing the "right" time to let go, to take risks, and to make decisions in the service of moving my writing forward.

Tip One: This work belongs to you!

Making Choices — The Thesis Topic

In the beginning, I was no different than most researchers/ writers who anxiously contemplate what to write about and how to proceed with the daunting task ahead. Indeed, even before I began to think what and how, I had to come to some understanding about why I wanted to write a thesis. What did a thesis mean to me? A thesis had always seemed a lofty pursuit which lay beyond my realm of accomplishment. Instead, in its practiced reality, I found it to be a very earthy enterprise, like everyday life — grounded in ordinary routines, conflicts, decision-making, and hard work. Reflecting on my initial indecision and self-doubt, I am somewhat embarrassed to admit that I went through three different topics, three proposals, two different methodologies, and three different committees before I finally settled on and felt committed to my final topic.

In retrospect, I view that very intense and frightening pre-writing period of floundering and "trying out" questions and methodologies as necessary sideroads on the path to discovering, trusting, and implementing "my way." What I eventually realized in the process of choosing an appropriate thesis topic was the importance of feeling connected to my subject and my project. I could not, nor did I desire to, put my life on hold and summon up sheer will power in service of a disenfranchised task; rather, I needed to align my will with my enquiry and to become a full participant in the act of "creating a thesis," to be committed to the task as well as the process, and to be open to the transitions and demands of the journey. Eventually, I found it beneficial to choose a topic that truly held a legitimate question for me, a question that energized my thinking, constantly pulled on my curiosity, and had the ability to draw the enquiry forward for six years: What is the nature and context of gender-related discrimination in the workplace? At its conception, I found my topic compelling because the experience of gender-related discrimination touched my life personally.

Eventually, my work received additional impetus and

charge from the discovery and poignancy of the experiences of others.

In its final (and arduously arrived at) embodiment, the thesis analyzes the experiences of six established and respected professional women who were confronted with persistent and systematic manifestations of subtle and covert discrimination in their workplaces. Although each woman's experiences, which included cumulative incidents of marginalization, isolation, silencing, devaluation, sabotage, harassment, exploitation, and manipulation, were difficult to identify, their impact was often felt by them to be more devastating than overt and often actionable forms of workplace discrimination. In fact, all eventually felt forced to leave their jobs. That I have received interest in and offers to publish my thesis suggests that I was able to strike a public nerve in my analysis of the astounding and heroic experiences of these women.

> **Tip Two: In choosing a topic balance**
> **your depth of interest and knowledge**
> **of the topic with your sense of its**
> **relevance and feasibility.**

Resolving Audience Tension

While struggling with my internal fears and anxieties, I found myself increasingly plagued by a seemingly unshakable albatross — the critical and imagined audience that was assigned to evaluate my expertise and to pounce on every indiscretion that I might commit. In fact, the notion of such a "daunting audience" haunted me and became a major force to be reckoned with throughout most of my thesis — truly a formidable, persistent and annoying interference on one hand, yet, in its less exaggerated normative form, offering an important legitimate perspective and backdrop against which most of my decisions, particularly those having to do with form and writing, were based. My ultimate goal was, after all, to communicate my work.

At first, I perceived my audience mainly in terms of my thesis supervisor who had perhaps the most familiarity with my thinking and my work. I was already accustomed to the intellectual exchange that existed at this level of writer-reader communication. Complications with my perception of audience surfaced as I increased the numbers in the audience and began to address the concerns or the imagined concerns of my thesis committee. In reality, my committee members were always supportive and seldom doubted the purpose and direction of my work. Nevertheless, I still struggled with my ambivalence about my ability to "please" and "appease" this growing "daunting" audience. Also, looming just beyond this small group were the judging and evaluating amorphous chorus of other scholars, critics, and people. Testing the reality of my projections with three constructive and generous committee members, however, was a pivotal step in my working through to a deeper and gradual realization that I could and must access and trust my own judgement and begin to chart my own path towards becoming my own expert. The resolution of this dialectic involving my thesis committee was pivotal in releasing my energy in readiness of being able to communicate to a legitimate larger audience while being less encumbered by my own "self-consciousness." My sense of empowerment to communicate grew steadily as I resolved not to allow myself to be held hostage by the presence of the notion of a "daunting audience." Indeed, I was invigorated by the realization that through my research and writing I was acquiring and accepting the right to have my say.

Tip Three: You can't please everyone
so you might as well please yourself.

Establishing Levels of Support

My thesis supervisor and committee were not only the testing ground for resolving my interaction with the "daunting audience" but also my first level of support in what would become an extensive network of resources. I chose a thesis committee that turned out to be a well-wishing, unobtrusive, non-competitive, truly professional and respectful team, each of whom in a unique way helped to midwife my expertise and competence. Specifically, the feedback and reassurance that I received from my supervisor and committee helped me to establish the boundaries within which to contain my work and to ignite my thought process when I reached moments of intellectual impasse.

A second level of support came rather unexpectedly in the second year of my research work when I became part of a "thesis support group" consisting of two other women who were working on their own theses and experiencing the same frustrations and anxieties as I. While the expertise of this group did not match that of the supervisor and committee, the members had useful ideas, data, and bibliographic information to share with each other. We also served as a much needed sounding board for each other and periodically monitored each other's progress. An important feature of this group was the formality of its structure and operation. We convened regular structured meetings (at least every two weeks throughout the intense formulating and collection period during the five years that we were together) in which some report was expected from each of us. I realized how important it was for me to be placed in a context of other writers and researchers, people who were doing the same things and struggling with similar concerns. Moreover, the mild competitiveness among us served to keep us "moving" for fear of being left behind. Most of us finished within a year of each other, and we are still friends today.

I found additional support in an informal network of writers and editors who not only made me more aware of the dynamics of writing a voluminous work but also connected me to a more general audience whom I eventually realized would also be interested in what I had to say. Often, they helped to set the direction for important revisions. No less important in serving as a barometer of audience reaction were an assortment of other friends and colleagues, whose informal and persistent presence in my life buoyed my spirits and, sometimes, flagging energies.

Despite the added expense, I felt supported by hiring occasional secretarial help. Although engaged primarily in mechanical duties (transcribing and cutting and pasting operations), her presence and efforts allowed me to feel that the work was not "piling up" during critical phases and allowed me to experience the continuity of progress and the camaraderie of teamwork. A more technical support which eventually became my constant companion was my laptop computer. It functioned as an efficient extension of my mind — rewrite as you go — with its ever-expanding "orphan" file of rejected but stored information for which I hoped to find a home later in the manuscript.

In the final analysis, writing a thesis seemed to me to be more a team effort than an individual, isolated enterprise. Although I was still the main player in a scholarly drama with the ultimate responsibility for production, the supporting players provided a normative context and, ultimately, a witness for my journey towards the maturation of my own expertise.

> **Tip Four: Build a support network**
> **that allows writing-research to**
> **become a normative and a team**
> **experience rather than an**
> **isolated performance.**

Arriving At Your Own Methodological Decisions

In working on a thesis, one inevitably confronts (sometimes for the first time) methodological tensions that must be resolved if the research is to bear fruit. As I had investigated volumes of qualitative methodological literature, looking for external directions — a kind of "how to" map — I grew quite disoriented and overwhelmed in my quest for the "one right methodology." After much agonizing and second guessing, I gave myself permission to become my own research methodologist. When I came to view the other established researchers as "supports" rather than "directors," I was able to maintain a better dynamic dialectical relationship with the research question as it evolved and to draw on several relevant outside supports as seemed necessary at each phase of the research process. During this process, I was forced squarely into declaring the roots of my thinking — my biases and my epistemological position with its established notions of knowledge, reliability, generalization, validity, subjectivity, objectivity, and unequivocal truth — and into challenging my lingering but tenacious traditional views about what was considered to be "good and hygienic science." Eventually, my study was guided by the influences and writings of heuristic, feminist, grounded theory, hermeneutical, and sociological researchers.

A second methodological tension emerged from my strong reservations about the barrier that language can create in the full explication and representation of experience. From my psychotherapy background where I had come to appreciate the efficacy of capturing "moments" in images and symbols, I decided to introduce an exercise in the interview protocol which would evoke spontaneous "imagaic statements." This activity within the interview gave each of the participants an opportunity to capture the essence of their experiences without having the pressure of formulating concepts in order to convey meaning. Ultimately, this innovation helped significantly in crafting the core analytical thematics.

A third methodological tension evolved from the fact that I was a participant in my own study. I felt pushed to examine the amount of distance that might be necessary — how close, how far — between myself, the researcher, and myself, the participant, in order to assure and stimulate new and critical understanding in the thesis analysis. After much reflection on this dialectic, I chose, despite the cost of extra time and effort, to deal with myself as a participant the way I did the other participants. I was interviewed by a colleague using the same protocol as had been used with the other participants. I also transcribed my own interview verbatim and, like the other participants, I referred to myself by a pseudonym throughout while keeping a running diary of my reactions to and insights about the transcript. This allowed me to view myself as separate from myself and as a part of the phenomenon under investigation.

Indeed, the resolution of these and other methodological tensions offered me a more relevant framework for my investigation and critical reflections. From there, I was able to proceed with the lengthy process of information gathering, a phase which generated further tensions, this time related to data management and analysis.

Tip Five: Let your thesis question
determine your methodological
choices.

Managing and Critically Analyzing the Research Data

An important discovery for me regarding data management and analysis was its non-linearity. In the course of data collection, it became vital for me to accept and manage the increasing number of overlapping activities that were beginning to occur. All activities dove-tailed and informed the others. It was especially important for me to accept that data overload and emotional and intellectual chaos are inevitable. Allowing chaos, holding tensions, being overwhelmed, making decisions, letting go ideas, avoiding polarization, altering cozy routines, allowing sufficient incubation time for ideas, all forced me to be responsive to the demands of the research question at any given moment. In the end, I was surprised how intimately I had come to know my research material, and I felt confident that I had reached the satiated point of knowing where the data was fundamentally leading me.

In the later phase of data management and analysis, I began to consider how my voluminous research notes could begin to be transformed into coherent and meaningful prose. After much resistance, I decided to follow the urging of an editorial advisor to construct a formal, detailed outline. I had always assumed that this effort, which the reader never sees, was a waste of time and that a loose and flexible informal guideline would be sufficient. To my amazement, however, the effort and time I put into creating a detailed formal outline came to represent one of the most time-efficient decisions, I made and proved to be a turning point in my work. Working out such a formal and detailed plan forced me to come to grips with the order, emphasis, and subordination of my chaotic collection of facts and ideas. The outline proved to be at once a focusing, researching, and planning instrument which gave me a greater sense of freedom to write.

**Tip Six: Allow ideas and insights to
emanate out of emotional and
intellectual chaos, and allow time
for reflection and revision.**

Developing a Writing Strategy

My discovery of the outline certainly instilled in me a clearer conception of the relationship between content and form in writing. I had previously viewed writing in terms of stream of consciousness or a spontaneous expression of artistic flair. Having had to confront the various tensions in my own thesis journey, however — relating to my focus, my sense of audience and my choices of methodological directions — I began to appreciate the interconnected nature of the various research and writing tasks. While working out an overall plan enhanced my organizational vision of the body of my work, learning about the value of introductions and conclusions helped me to adhere to the conceptual unity of my argument in the whole thesis and within each chapter and section. Overall, I came to realize and accept that the task of writing involved much more than just having something interesting to say. It invariably involved the strategic mobilization of a multitude of resources (facts and ideas) to achieve a concrete and vibrant representation of a personal intellectual vision.

Tip Seven: Take as much time to organize as to write.

Preparing to Defend: Claiming Your Expertise

As a result of the resolution of so many emotional and intellectual tensions, by the time my thesis defense came about, I felt a strong sense of personal integration and scholarly growth. Feeling unusually comfortable in my intimate knowledge of the various dimensions of my research topic, I approached the preparation for my thesis defense with the attitude that I would probably never be in quite this space of accomplishment about this topic again. So, I asked myself how I wanted to best represent myself and my work in this moment of ending my apprenticeship and claiming my expertise.

I chose as integrated and innovative an approach to my defense as I had to my thesis. While I spent time preparing the content of my defense, I concentrated equally on the attitude I would bring to, and the process by which I would present, my work. In particular, I wanted to remain "present" to the occasion of my defense. I did not want to miss a moment of this opportunity to celebrate and discuss my work. For me, the defense was, and continues to remain a significant and poignant event of my life.

So, in the end, it indeed became more "practical" — at least in terms of my ultimate sense of accomplishment and satisfaction — for me to be aligned with both myself and my thesis. While I watched others try to put their lives on hold in order to survive the process, every part of me protested attempts to make my thesis an academic exercise in "will power." In hindsight, I know I would have been very disappointed had I tried to short circuit and bypass my total involvement in my work with its various sideroads of discovery, tension and resolution. In the end, because of the ultimate meaning that "forging" my unique path through to its final production had for me, my thesis endeavor became an exquisite and liberating experience.

Tip Eight: Carpe diem — seize the moment !!!

From Numbers to Words

C. T. Patrick Diamond

Thesis Title:

**Constructs, Practices and Effects of
Teaching Written Expression**

Unpublished doctoral thesis,
University of Queensland, Brisbane, 1979.

When I Was a Traveller: How I Got There Myself

I find that I can best help others to "get there" with their
thesis research by continuing to reflect on how I got there
myself. My journey has led me from words to numbers
and then on to words again. With the aid of many guides
and maps, I have travelled from literary beginnings
through empirical procedures to narrative inquiry.

I first got into trouble for preferring words to numbers in
elementary school in Australia. It was my favorite day of
the week when we were allowed to borrow from the library.
I couldn't wait to start my new book, not about expatriate
writers in Tangier but about the exploits of Indians on the
Plains. So, during the next lesson (which happened to be
math), after I had finished the allotted tasks, I opened the
book only to be told to put it away. Undeterred, I completed all the set problems in that chapter of the textbook.
I tried reading again but under the desk. Then I really "got
it." Who did I think I was? Did I think it was up to me to
decide what I wanted to do?

After graduating to a day boys' high school, I sensed that
I wanted to become a traveller. I spent the first school
weekend anxiously polishing up a composition set for
homework. I wrote about a bear attack and was later taken
by surprise to hear my new form master read it out to the

class, analysing its successes. He said that I had begun "in medias res." In Latin, I learned that Virgil used this technique as well. Tacit knowledge of my own practice became explicit knowledge of that of others. But it took thirty more years for me to learn that we begin thesis research not in the middle but at the end. We have to imagine what the real question is that we eventually want to answer.

In 1979, on the recommendations of my external thesis examiners, Jimmy Britton and Janet Emig, I was awarded my PhD. The three page abstract, like the thesis, was written in the third person, in the past tense, and mainly in the passive voice. It now reminds me of a campus novel with a cast of shadowy players. What had seemed like a clash of personalities I now recognize as tension between different research agenda; however, any one of them can provide only an approximation to knowledge. I am still trying to understand the dilemmas that my research led me to. Compared to the original thesis of 559 pages, I prefer the recent two paragraph account that I give in a chapter on teacher change (Diamond, 1993).

I completed my master's thesis, part-time over two years, while lecturing in English Language and Literature at a teachers' college. Since it was a research thesis, there was no coursework. My supervisor was head of the University's Department of Education and chair of its Educational Psychology strand. I had already taught for five years after completing a Bachelor's degree in Arts and training as a high school teacher of English and History. One of the Bachelor of Education courses that I took with the head introduced me to theories of personality, including George Kelly's (1955) psychology of personal constructs.

In my undergraduate studies and in my later teaching, I was mainly interested in what critics called the psychological novel. I was curious about the role of the narrator, especially in the work of Henry James and James Joyce where they struggled to represent consciousness. On the advice of the employing authority to "do something with learning in it," I had also taken undergraduate courses in psychology, including the obligatory statistics and experimental design. The head of psychology warned us that it was not the subject to study if we wanted to find out more about ourselves. I turned increasingly to education. The research of its head (and hence my master's thesis) focused on achievement motivation (n.Ach.) and independent study. He had been awarded a research grant to study the effects of the provision of high school libraries by the federal government.

After being appointed to the Department of Education as a lecturer in English Curriculum and Instruction, I was enrolled in the doctoral program. This consisted entirely of thesis — no course work, no comprehensive examinations, no supportive group of other candidates, no thesis committee, just the candidate and supervisor for however long it took. I felt that I wanted to do something about how teachers taught writing or written composition. After decades of research, I wondered how English teachers, including those that I had helped to prepare, could still cling to teaching formal Latinate grammar. Perhaps they would learn to see writing differently only by writing themselves?

My former English Curriculum and Instruction lecturer volunteered to be my doctoral supervisor. He was beginning to teach courses in social learning theory in Educational Psychology. After he accepted a post at another university, he arranged for me to be supervised by a professor who had returned to the department after an appointment at OISE. This supervisor had been a high school math teacher, a math curriculum lecturer in the department, then a senior lecturer in psychology, a psychometrician at OISE, and finally, a professor in educational psychology. This is one track that classroom teachers travel on their way to becoming thesis guides.

I began studying (measuring) how ninety-three teachers from twenty-two high schools thought about the teaching of writing. My contribution to the research design lay in seeking to understand their practices by constructing fifteen intensive case studies of them during the school year. I was advised to study also the effects of their pedagogy on the achievement of their 372 students. It was only later that I recognized this design as teacher effectiveness research. In a sea of variables, numbers and matrices, I clung to the raft provided by the actual words of the teachers as I interviewed them in schools. I most wanted to understand their intentions and how these meshed with their practices. After five years, still lecturing in the department, I had completed the data collection, recognized the "natural breaks" in the numerous multivariate displays, and so turned in a final draft; however, with all its "non-significant differences," the research did not feel like me. There was more that needed to brought out from "under the desk."

After the thesis was forwarded to the newly elected head, a sociologist, he made only two comments. My conceptual framework was too linear and I had consistently misspelt "hierarchical." Then some kind of shadow drama was played out against a paradigmatic (or political) backdrop. The thesis was next forwarded to the former head (my master's supervisor) who was still a force in the department. He read it closely over the weekend and phoned for us to meet. He advised that I should take another year to refocus and rewrite. I should "bite the bullet." What I had written read more like a measurement exercise than a meaning-based thesis. I needed to go back and resurface my own implicit theories and those of the teachers. What had underpinned my major research decisions? Wasn't I really interested in understanding teachers' constructs and why they taught as they did? What was more measurable had driven the more important out of the thesis. To do the "re-search," I needed to backtrack and change perspectives. I chose a group of scholars to be my guides (and referees) for the next ten years. They, and others, provided guideposts for a subsequent book in which I used Repertory grid and narrative approaches to explore teacher education as transformation of perspective (Diamond, 1991).

If I had completed my first doctoral draft as a tourist, I resubmitted it as a traveller. It was not just that I preferred working with words rather than numbers. I learned to speak in my own voice and not to sacrifice my intentions to those of others. I had to find my own forms, negotiating other ways of representing the teachers' classroom experiences. The difference is also partly one of time. The tourist just wants the thesis "done" and hurries home as soon as possible. In contrast, the traveller stays "out there," on the margins, accepting research as a way of life. Research travellers (and guides) take responsibility for their processes, including intuition. They cast their nets widely, letting them down into promising waters.

Many beginning travellers feel that their experience needs to be legitimated by appeals to the published authority of others. They want to portray their ideas as just fitting in with the literature. In constructing Repertory grid and narrative case studies of teachers' practice (and especially my own), I realized that actual practice outstrips explicit theory. We do not have to wait to measure, or even to name, something before we explore it. In the thesis process, you, the candidate, will know best what you should look for, what questions you should ask, and what methods you should use. And this is particularly so at the end of your study. The process of getting to the end will take you through terrain that, while growing more complex and detailed, will eventually become clearer as a whole. You will make it through the thesis, with yourself providing the source of its best ideas.

Now That I Am Also a Guide: Helping Others to Get There

In 1986, Ortrun Zuber-Skerritt and I studied how a group of graduate students, who completed a formal, "outside in" course on learning to do research, still felt that they were only poor researchers. They could not get past thinking that what they needed was a rigid, predetermined plan with null hypotheses sealed in an envelope. While they believed that doing a thesis also demanded that they learn to become good managers both of time and data, what they needed was to begin with and to make the best use of themselves. To become thesis travellers, tourists must acquire personal knowledge and improvise with map-making.

I now work individually and with groups of my thesis students who form their own additional response trios or support groups. We also share a course on educational research that focuses on them as they prepare the pro-posal or complete the thesis. Previously, I had labored the differences between the psychometric, phenomenological, sociolinguistic, and narrative highways in the research landscape. But I now realize that it is only when a task, such as doing a thesis, makes human sense that we can carry it out successfully, finding new paths.

Since so many candidates ask if what they are doing could really constitute research, I begin by asking them to consider themselves as if they were researchers ("If I were a researcher, I ...") and their proposal or thesis as if it were research ("If my thesis were research,..."). To become more research-sighted, they ask themselves: "What if my re-search became...?" and "How is my research going?" They draw maps of their thesis journeys and keep journals or logs, describing their research practices and reflecting on them. They write about preferred research methods and explore how these reflect personal choices which in turn connect with their life histories.

While discussing how personal and professional lives intersect, I share my writing with them as other work in progress. We use sentence starters, drawings, metaphors, and images to prompt narrative self-descriptions. These ways of getting a handle on our meaning making include: "How I came to my research...;" "As a thesis student, I...;" "The researcher I am...;" "The researcher I fear to become...;" and "The researcher I want to become...." Being blocked on a plateau is construed as an invitation to take risks and follow hunches that we may have been resisting. Being stuck provides an important staging point for re-hearsing for growth.

We constantly ask one another: "What do you most want to know about? What do you really want to do?" Such invitations help us put anxieties aside and clear a space for self-exploration and group collaboration. We tap into our non-propositional modes of understanding and look for our individual, signature patterns. New patterns can then be created. Since different maps take us along different paths, we redraw or redirect our thesis journeys so that they can lead to a visualized pot of gold or a rainbow rather than to a hanged man ("just one more rewrite"), to a wide sargasso sea (always becalmed so that "nothing helps"), or to an ancient mariner, eternally wandering as ABD ("all but dissertation" completed). By representing and redirecting our felt sense of the proposal or thesis, we can check where we are and, if needed, change the tack we have taken.

Many candidates initially seem to be lacking in research confidence or wary of the thesis as just another exercise in conformity; however, no one can tell them which question or topic to pursue. Only they can create the meanings for the thesis to convey. Ironically, many of these reluctant researchers have already worked as teachers of gifted students, devising and negotiating enriching programs of independent study, expertly helping to equip others with methods of inquiry to investigate real life problems. And so, I ask them to consider themselves as gifted students ("As a gifted learner doing a thesis, I...;") and then to plan the thesis as a journey leading to their transformation. Although examining authorities require that a thesis "makes an original contribution to knowledge," research just as importantly changes what and how we know.

I am interested in following previously hidden paths that take the thesis in the direction of narrative or the novel, reflexive genres in which self can be interrogated as the composing author. We ask of each thesis chapter: "Who is (are) doing the talking?" and "How did this happen?" The recollected stories of how each of the candidates came to their topics provide important issues to be addressed as part of the proposal and thesis.

We are all researchers and inquiry itself is an everyday activity. We need to approach our thesis topic as closely as clinicians and to invite our participants to join with us in investigating the problem. All our tentative answers contribute to the refinement of the questions that originally launched them. Advances in understanding come from raising new questions as possibilities and from relooking at old questions from other angles.

Tips for Guides

- Remember your own tourist and travelling days.
- How can your students' theses make better human sense?
- Explore the connections between your research choices and your life history.
- Find students whose research interests match yours.
- What stories do their theses tell of your growth?

Tips for Travellers

- Though you may begin as a tourist, you will become a traveller and map your own course.
- The proposal or thesis has to feel like you. It has to make good human sense.
- What real question interests you most? What do you want to do?
- Find the connections between your research and your life history.
- Find other researchers whose interests match yours. Read and interview them about their work.
- Find likely guides.
- Become your own best guide.

- Begin at the end. What is the question that you want to answer?
- Keep a journal. Reflect on your preferred research processes and personal choices.
- What are your signature patterns?
- Rewrite and reconsider your thesis or report.
- Your research will change what and how you know.
- Get a fresh perspective.

Tips for Tourists

- Before coming to research, you should be inoculated for the length of the journey; lessen your reliance on the authority of others; and say goodbye to your lack of confidence in self, and to any hope for an ultimate guidebook. Once you begin, resist the urge to hurry home to the safety of the known. You can become a traveller only by staying "out there," on the margins. And you will arrive.

The Creation of a Thesis:
An Inner and Outer Story

Laura Ford

Thesis Title:

The Creation of Settings: An Inquiry Into the Early Years of the York Faculty of Education

Unpublished doctoral thesis,
University of Toronto, 1992.

My thesis brought me to a journey back in time. The inquiry into the creation of the York Faculty of Education is told through the voices of its three early participants. And one of the stories is mine. How were our ideas born? What bothered us and made us struggle over the issues? Interviewed for the New York Review of Books, Isaiah Berlin says, "To write a good illuminating history. . . you must try to see these problems from the 'inside'. . . . You must try to enter into what the ideas meant to those who entertained them" [The New York Review of Books, "Philosophy and Life: An Interview": May 28, 1992, p.50]. The York story is a story of the times, starting from the mid-sixties to the early seventies, as it is formed in the minds of the narrators in the early nineties, twenty years later. It is about a time in the history of the educational community and it is about a personal time in the lives of the three individuals.

Writing a thesis demands originality in identifying and researching its subject, and for me it also was being a subject of the research, inquiring into my experiences as a co-creator of a setting. What was common to both researcher and inquirer was finding the way of the *outer* and *inner* journey that was present in both places. And in the writing of the thesis I recognized that the tension I was experiencing was not only that of researcher and inquirer, but also that of writer.

A Thesis: The Creation of a Setting

I recall sitting in on seminars listening to individuals discuss their thesis-in-progress. I could understand little of the passion they exhibited until I found myself in the process of writing my own thesis. Writing a thesis is an experience in crafting and creating; the thesis finds its form from an inner place the writer knows in tension with the expectations set down by the academic community. The thesis holds a truth that becomes known in its writing; the search to finding one's way brings together the insights and wisdom of other scholars combined with one's own experiences and knowing.

The writing of a thesis creates its own setting. When I first began to reflect on the phrase the *creation of settings* my thoughts turned me to my personal stories and the settings I created for myself. And today I look back on my thesis journey, the three years in which I travelled its course, as the *creation of a setting*. The creation of a thesis embraces the inner creative spirit and the crafting of the art to give expression to that creativity. One continuously travels the inner and outer pathways that one finds for oneself, not unlike a stream finding its own course.

Beginning with Myself through Imagery

Our entrance into any place begins with ourselves (Hunt, 1987), that which resides in our hearts, heads, and actions. And, as I began to lay out the stories of my journey, I found my way by stepping from stone to stone and moving into the stones. As I tripped along my way I came upon images and textures and words which gained new meanings. The path I was taking led me to a specific end that, until the writing, was not known to me. I found along the way a personal image that accompanied me and continues to work its way through the different callings of my life. The first recognition of my image came to me in the process of reading Tolstoy's *Anna Karenin* for a class in my undergraduate program. It was a course on the Great Books in which we were asked to critique the books we read.

I wrote about Levin in the field, dressed in white linens, moving the scythe in rhythm with his serfs and in rhythm

with the wind (Tolstoy, 1954, pp 269-272). I could hear
nothing else and could write on nothing else. It was the
beginning of a developing image that finds its threads in
my personal story and in my experienced knowledge.

The image that moves through my experienced knowledge is that of a field of wheat. I recognize the need to be
nourished by the soil and the sun in order for the sheaths
of wheat to achieve their growth so that they can be free in
their own movement The image was grounded in a particular experience that came with the purchase of our farm
in Puslinch, Ontario, one of the few remaining farm com-
munities within commuting distance to the city of Toronto.

The land had not been worked for many years and
twich, farmer's weeds, had taken over the soil. The only
way to recover the land was to apply atrozine to the soil.
This meant that only feed corn could grow on that land for
three years. For those three years I knew that in the
spring, when I looked out the window, I would see the
stalks of corn in rows, tall and straight and unbending. I
could barely wait until the soil was free from its twich and
free to feed whatever I chose to sow. Then I could plant my
wheat. My wheat held freedom, the freedom to feel and to
move, from within and without.

The image of my life comes to me in the form of corn
and wheat. There is the *corn* that represents that part of
my life that exists by meeting the necessities defined by
nature or man-made rules and guidelines. The *wheat*
represents my freedom of movement and personal expression. The wheat has to do with how I find myself. My
journey is a journey through the corn and the wheat. It is
a journey through teaching and learning, the mimetic
mode and the expressive mode, the crafting and the creating. The thesis journey held the corn and the wheat.

The Journey
I was in awe of the thesis process. I was knowing about
myself but unknowing about what was expected of me.
There was a great distance between those *inner* and *outer*
places. The unexpected led me to find my way. As the
traveller upon an unknown territory I sought out the
markings in the form of my thesis supervisor. He became
my guide. It was not that I leaned on him; rather, he
helped me find my balance. The unexpected was the extent of his belief that I could find my way. His belief in me

was never heard so loudly than in one of our meetings about my chapter on methodology.

I had spent hours resourcing myself with readings on phenomenology and hermeneutics. As I set the chapter to paper I was barely evident in the text. And my supervisor was looking for me and for what he knew of my work. I had sought out his acknowledgment for doing what I thought was expected and he turned me back onto my own knowing. I had been coming at the chapter from an *outer* place, not trusting my own learning and years of experience. I was stalking the chapter, coming at it stiffly as a stalk of corn and I held tightly to that posture. When all else failed to loosen my grip, my supervisor's humor set me free to respond to how I knew the material from an *inner place*. I finally described a methodology that enabled me to tell my story in its own way, in a way more exquisite to its task, more reflective of the movement of the sheaths of wheat.

I had over one hundred transcript pages of each of the participants telling their stories. For each participant's story I read and reread the pages and identified themes that came out of their recollections. I then cut up the pages of the transcripts and placed all of the individual's own words under appropriate headings. My floor looked like the editing room of a film company, but instead of pictures I had words — black lines on a white background to be put together from a script of its own making.

I was finding a new experience with the words as they were reframed under the headings that I had provided but that were suggested by the participants' words and thoughts. I was beginning to experience myself. I was reacting to the printed word on white sheets as I knew myself as artist with pen and ink on paper. The writing held the joys of a creative experience as the words took on the form of their story and found their own flow and meaning.

I began to focus on the meaning of "inner" and "outer" voice. I reached out to philosophy and Bergson's metaphysical writings (1955), to literary criticism and to Seamus Heaney's book, *Preoccupations, Selected Prose 1968-1978*. It was not that I could give meaning to all that I was reading, but there was a comfort in the meaning that I could take from their writings. It was during this time that I chose to reread Camus in preference to Sartre. Camus offers me an *inner* experience while I found Sartre outside his words.

Creating and Crafting a Thesis

Always present, but in the background as I was developing my thesis was Collingwood's work, *The Principles of Art* (1938). Collingwood distinguishes between "art and not art," crafts and "art proper" (Collingwood, 1938).

> Craft always involves a distinction between means and end, each clearly conceived as something distinct from the other but related to it. It in-volved a distinction between planning and execu-tion. The result to be obtained [in crafting] is preconceived or thought out before being arrived at. The craftsman [sic] knows what he wants to make before he makes it...the foreknowledge is not vague but precise. If a person sets out to make a table, but conceives the table only vaguely, as somewhere between two by four feet and three by six, and between two and three feet high, and so forth, he is no craftsman. (Collingwood, 1938 p.15-16)

The surprises lay not in the crafting but in the creating. Coming to a doctoral thesis through qualitative research both the crafting and creating hold their surprises as the subject finds its form.

Often I would find that I could only enter a chapter by beginning with a paragraph that I knew I would eventually set aside. I needed to begin there if only for myself. It was part of the process that I learned to accept in order to find my way. It was not unlike the blank canvas for the artist or the empty page for the poet. Qualitative research, though it maintains its own parameters, requires meaning making beyond the singleness of the scientific method and demands that the researcher be more active and creative in crafting the text. In thesis writing, as one moves into one's own work, there is a responsibility to be true to the thesis and true to oneself.

In choosing the topic of my thesis, the creation of set-tings, I recognized that the word "creation" held specific meaning. My thesis began to find its form from the book by Seymour Sarason, *The Creation of Settings and the Future Societies* (1972). Sarason might have chosen an-other phrase to give meaning to his thoughts and experi-ences, the "making" of a setting, for example, but he did not. So, taking Sarason's phrase seriously, I decided to enter into Sarason's subject with the intent to focus on the word "creation" and explore its presence and how it finds its meaning in the creation of settings. The New Webster's Dictionary defines creation with both the verbs "creating" and "making."

As I reached the final pages of my thesis I had come upon my own definition of the creation of settings. How we go about creating our settings begins with ourselves, finding our balance from within and without — corn and wheat implicit and explicit — inner and outer — masculine and feminine — and how we bring together our own voices so that we can hear ourselves and the voices of others is the story of the creation of settings. The creation of a setting is a continuous story. Sometimes we have to recognize when the canvas works and we can do nothing more to it without it becoming something else. There are choices. We can keep working on the old canvas or we may choose to take ourselves to a second canvas, and perhaps to a third. How can we design a canvas that allows for continuous new images and form?

The creation of a setting is the expression of its creators and each person who enters the setting is invited to become part of the creation. It is both an inner and outer experience. The inner experiences are the feelings and emotions, the knowing and the learning that is rooted in our personal histories; the outer experiences find the form to give voice to the inner experiences. That is the crafting and creating of a setting.

Reflections

I came to the graduate school knowing the professor I was going to approach to become my supervisor. I asked him to guide me through the creation of my thesis. He travelled with me. He walked with me on my pathway bringing his experienced knowledge. He helped me find the balance between the corn and the wheat. When I held tightly to the words of the hermeneutic methodologists and lost my balance to the outer voice, his guidance led me to trust my own methodology. There were times that I feared that my supervisor's voice was louder than my own. I let him hear my fears in the forms of painting and poetry. I was not unlike an adolescent rebelling against a parent's values before becoming a young adult.

The creation of a thesis embraces all those who enter its

domain. It embraces the writers of the texts that resource the researcher. It embraces the colleagues who are writing their own work. And, above all, it embraces the relation-ship between the traveller and guide.

I had just returned home from delivering the final ver-sion of my thesis to my committee. I had let the manu-script out of my hands. As I sat in front of my fireplace in late October, 1993, I turned to the front page of my copy and it was as if I were reading the thesis for the first time. It was mine. "Truth resides less in events than in the reverberation set by them; less in the single note than in the harmony produced by a combination of notes" (Nathan, 1961, p.140).

If I Can Do It, So Can You!

Dorothea Dobbs Gaither

Thesis Title:

An Exploration of the Experience of Using Guided Imagery to Prepare for Surgery

Unpublished doctoral thesis,
University of Toronto, 1993.

As I ended my doctoral course work and was preparing to write my thesis proposal, I was diagnosed with a herniated spinal disk. I spent three months confined to bed before surgery. I went from having great expectations of relief from my intense leg and back pain before surgery to the slow realization that I had become one of those who fit into the category called "Failed Back Surgery Syndrome." What this meant to my life was that pain became my constant companion. Sitting for more than ten minutes caused hours of intense pain. The challenge of the next four years of my life was to learn how to balance the needs of my fragile back with meeting my goal of conducting my research and writing my thesis. I began to live the paradox of feeling totally overwhelmed by the prospect of writing my thesis while I was in so much pain yet feeling motivated to try to cope with the pain *because* I had a thesis to write.

The old adage that "necessity is the mother of invention" came to life on a daily basis for me. For example, I wrote my thesis proposal lying flat on a bed in front of my computer with the keyboard propped up on a pillow on my stomach. During the analysis and writing phases, I had to find a way to take frequent breaks from sitting, but I kept becoming engrossed in the work. The solution was to buy a quartz kitchen timer. My whole thesis was written in fifteen minute segments with breaks in between to walk around and stretch. My physical limitations challenged me to " work smart," not just hard and to be creative, flexible, and non-linear in my problem solving.

The Joys and Excitement of the Journey

Initially, my interest in my thesis topic sprang from my own positive personal experience of using imagery techniques to prepare for abdominal surgery. Encouraged by the power of my own experience, I began to work with friends and acquaintances who sought me out to help them prepare for surgery. With each new experience, new questions begged to be investigated, and my respect grew for each individual's capacity to be led by an inner wisdom. Just like a child playing at the beach where land and water meet, I found myself drawn to explore the terrain where body and mind meet. This interest lasted through the whole thesis enterprise and continues today.

One of my greatest joys during the thesis journey was "saturating the literature." By this I mean that I read and read and read in the psychology, nursing, and medical literature in an ever-widening circle of topics to increase my understanding. At a certain point, although I knew I had not read absolutely everything on the subject, I realized that I was no longer encountering any new ideas or insights. For the first time in my academic career, I felt I had gleaned all the important ideas and data on a subject and knew that I had insights that went beyond what was found in the current literature. The joy came from standing on the frontier of what was already known and what was yet to be explored and discovered.

In several of the qualitative methodology books that I read, the authors encouraged researchers to refrain from talking about their work during the analysis and writing process. My understanding of this suggestion is that the creative energy needed for reflection and writing could be released or dissipated by discussing the work; however, for me, the exact opposite was true. I always felt encouraged when friends, family, colleagues, and total strangers found my topic interesting. Talking about the ongoing research always excited me and helped me stay connected to my own passion. Finally, I believe I often became clearer in my understanding while I was speaking to others about my topic. The act of sending out words to caring listeners helped me, in a sense, to hear myself think out loud, edit, and rework ideas.

When the Going Gets Tough, the Tough Get Organized!

Watching other doctoral students run into time-consuming and energy-consuming procedural, logistical, and methodological roadblocks encouraged me to take time before beginning my research to plan my strategy with the hope of avoiding some of the pitfalls. My early slogan was; "If it is worth doing, then it is worth thinking about first."

My very first step was to identify my own learning style and work style. Taking time for this self-examination helped in several ways. For example, I realized that I am a social creature and have never been very creative when isolated. With this knowledge, I sought out the company and support of several fellow doctoral students. My three "study buddies" had different thinking styles and skills that often complimented rather than mirrored my own style and skill. Developing these long-term supportive relationships allowed me to feel connected to others who also were walking the lonely thesis road. We supported and challenged each other in many ways. We often found references and quotes for each other, helped by listening and asking questions to clarify thinking, and gave each other constructive feedback and suggestions.

One time when I felt that I had hit an impasse, one of these colleagues came over with large pieces of poster paper and colored markers. She told me to talk about the problem. As I spoke, she put down major words and concepts, "doodled", and drew arrows. At the end of an hour of talking it out, I understood the problem much better; I had diagrams that helped organize my thinking; and I found a way to break out of my linear thinking of either/or to find a third and better solution.

Another planning strategy that I employed was to think ahead and picture myself working on my thesis. This helped me anticipate what I needed to get and do before I started. Products of this planning process were the realizations that I needed a space of my own to conduct my research and write the thesis and an adequate data management system. A small home renovation created a very comfortable and inviting office in my basement. After creating the office, I established two filing systems. One was a hard copy filing system to help keep the huge amount of research data in an order that could be used with ease. Files included folders for transcripts, field notes, journals, new questions, references, notes from meetings with my thesis supervisor, hunches, etc. The other was a system to organize the many computer files and disks that would be needed to conduct the study. Early in the process, I researched and chose the potential word processing functions, like "cut and paste" and "sort", that I might need. This helped me choose the computer software that was powerful enough to carry me through the whole research project.

Through the whole time that I was working on my thesis I practised what I call "good computer hygiene." By this I mean I took care to follow certain procedures that protected my data such as frequently "saving" material on a floppy disk, having a different disk for each participant's transcripts and for each chapter, making two back-up disks for each disk, and keeping a set of disks on a different floor from my office. Taking the time to create and maintain an organized system helped me to feel in control of the growing data and my process.

Another decision that helped me to organize and clarify my thinking was to conduct and analyze a pilot study. This activity helped me make major decisions about the design of the study. Some of the decisions included the procedures I would follow with my participants, the kind of atmosphere that was needed for the pre-surgery imagery sessions, the kinds of questions I would ask in the post-operative interviews, and the amount of flexibility that was required of me to be able to meet the needs of each individual participant.

Digging In and Doing It!

Four time management strategies that I would recommend while working on a thesis are: (1) make a time-line; (2) break the large task into smaller ones; (3) edit as you go along; and, (4) alternate types of tasks. Without a time-line, it is very easy to use as much time as there is and to lose sight of where you are in the process. The time-line needs to be flexible, but taking the time to determine the order of things and estimating how long different tasks might take will help you be clear and realistic. The thought of writing a thesis is daunting, to say the least;

however, the idea of writing a chapter feels more "do-able." Breaking the project up into smaller, more manageable pieces which are being accomplished creates an ongoing sense of accomplishment.

Once the writing has started, try putting the material down for short periods of time and then returning to read it with an objective eye. I spent time editing by reading for content, simplicity, clarity, and style. When I finished writing my last chapter, I only had the table of contents and the acknowledgments to do, since I had edited the thesis and updated my reference list as I went along.

The saying, "A change is as good as a rest" can not only be very true, it can be time and energy efficient when working on a thesis. I found I could get more work done each day if I did not ask myself to do the same kind of task for long periods of time. For example, I might work on an analysis of a transcript for several hours and then read other theses or material for the literature review. After my daily journalling, where I tried to capture new questions and insights as they occurred to me, I might transcribe, code, analyze, write, or edit.

Consider a Quote Bank

While writing several term papers during my master's program, I experienced frustration from occasionally being unable to find an exact quote I needed, a page number, or all the information for the reference list. To prevent this frustration and the wasting of time, I got into the habit of creating a computer file of all quotes that I thought I might use along with the necessary publishing information. Toward the end of my doctoral course work, I began to understand how much material I would read while working on my thesis. The potential to forget where I had read something or to not be able to find a quote or reference that I needed encouraged me to expand my habit of keeping a "quote bank." Although it took an initial investment of time to type in all the quotes I found of interest from all the material I read, this habit created a rich resource during the writing process. The added benefit was that I never had to return to the original books, since I had all the information I needed on file.

Wrestling with Fear

Even though I had been a successful graduate student

who had written many term papers and had worked as a copy editor and assistant editor, I approached the writing of my doctoral thesis with a deep sense of insecurity about my writing ability. The fear was not rational, but it was extremely strong. Using several strategies helped me prevent writer's paralysis. First, after imaging the finished product, I decided that the two qualities that I wanted my thesis to embody were simplicity and clarity. These two words were posted right above my computer throughout the whole writing process to keep me grounded in my writing style goal. Second, I tried to read one doctoral thesis about every two weeks. Although some of them made me feel truly humble, others encouraged me to believe that I could produce a thesis because they, too, were less than perfect. Being exposed to so many studies helped calm my fear by demystifying the process for me. The third step I took to handle my insecurity about writing was to adjust my attitude by giving myself permission to be playful and to write anything in any way. By this I mean that I kept reminding myself that I could edit, change, or scrap anything I wrote. Another writing aid was to continually ask myself "How does this story want to be told?" I was often surprised when an answer came back which seemed to lead me in the right direction. Finally, there is no substitute for a reality check. I enlisted my husband and a few friends as readers. Using them as guinea pigs, I was able to see their reactions to the content, as well as to my writing style. Their comments and support helped my trust grow in my ability as a researcher and writer.

Final Thoughts and Thanks

A whole chapter could be written about my experience with my thesis supervisor. Let me summarize it by saying that I am deeply grateful to my thesis supervisor for believing in me and my ability and for always charging me with the task of being true to myself, the data, and the process. Rather than showing me the way, my thesis supervisor inspired the confidence in me that I needed to find my own way.

By the time the day of my final defense arrived, I felt that I also "had arrived." A subtle transformation had taken place in me during the thesis enterprise. I identify the two sides of my student persona before my thesis as "arrogant" and "scared." At my defense the two sides had evolved into "humble" and "secure." In a very real sense, I had become willing to "own" my strengths as well as my weaknesses, and to value my process as well as my accomplishment.

Things you might find Helpful in the Thesis Journey

Preparation
- Take time to identify your own learning and work style.
- Take time to think through data organization and demands of your probable process.
- Set up a filing system on paper and on your computer.
- Take time to make a supportive physical environment.
- The pilot study can help you refine your study design and anticipate potential snags.

Organization
- Develop a quote bank. From the very beginning of the process, copy quotes with all the reference information. You might not use all the quotes, but you will never have   to go back to the primary material.
- Field notes and journals are important places to capture insights, hunches, and emerging patterns...later they can help you retrace your own process.
- When transcribing or analysing data on the computer, consider working in two documents to capture your reactions to the data in the moment.
- Make a time-line! This helps you estimate the time needed and to break up the project into do-able pieces.
- Have a variety of different tasks that you can work on so you can change tasks without stopping work (write/edit, read/journal, transcribe/organize material).

What Helped Me
- I collected names of thesis authors from those

whose opinions I respected and read a thesis every two weeks. I collected ideas I liked in terms of style, format, methodology, etc.

- I worked with 3 "study buddies."
- I always was asking myself: What am I learning? What is interesting and where am I being led by the data?
- When I got stuck, I tried to break out of linear thinking.
- I edited as I went along, so there was very little to do after I wrote the last chapter.
- When outlining, imagine how the thesis will look... ask how does this story want to be told?
- I often taped myself talking about the thesis. I got clearer when I talked about it.
- I spent almost equal time on the thesis content and the process.

Remember
- A thesis is like writing 15 term papers!
- Take time to get some distance so you can see the big picture.
- Don't just work hard —WORK SMART!
- Do what you have to do to stay in touch with your enthusiasm.

Back to the Future

George L. Geis

Thesis Title:

**Matching to Sample by Retarded Children:
The Effects of Delayed Response and
Number of Alternatives**

Unpublished doctoral dissertation, Columbia University, 1965.

Almost any assignment that returns me to my youth is welcome these days. Going back to my time as a graduate student some 40 years ago, has brought mostly smiles and warm feelings. More importantly, it has revealed some things that I learned about carrying out a thesis research that may be useful to others today.

I started a thesis project at Columbia University where I was a graduate student in Psychology. The focus was on the area of *variability* in human responses: what affects it? Numerous discrete responses can be classified into a single category because they look alike, occur under similar circumstances, and have the same effects on the environment. Yet every time we emit a particular response (say, opening a door) it differs somewhat from a similar response emitted at another time. If we keep saying the same word aloud, we can detect clear variations in the responses. Trying to maintain uniformity of response requires enormous effort as, for example, the professional pianist knows when attempting to replicate a performance. So, I wondered what were some of the influences on this phenomenon? More particularly I was interested in what happens when the consequences of the response were varied. Thus: if one had been rewarded for making a particular response and then the rewards suddenly were stopped, what would happen to the topography of that response? It was (and still is) a neat question and of some importance in an analysis of human behavior.

I chose as my response a rather simple human vocal utterance: the "o-o-o" sound as in "Who" and "Shoe". I won't go into the reasons for its choice but there were a lot of good ones. The subjects were asked to sit in a darkened chamber and to detect whether or not the needle on a meter before them was deflected from the middle point on the dial. They were given money for each correct detection. The catch was that they could illuminate the dial briefly only by uttering the designated sound.

I went through the usual convolutions of designing such a study: the control group, the formative testing of apparatus and subjects, and so on. The response was, in fact, a complicated thing to analyze, requiring very sophisticated equipment and extremely precise environmental controls. And the data obtained forced me into even more complicated activities. Daily I became increasingly bogged down — if the apparatus worked (which it frequently did not) the sounds from outside the area contaminated the data. If the room was quiet, the analysis of the data was proving more and more intractable. One day after my last, patient "o-o-oer" had left the booth, I realized that the whole task was well beyond both me and the equipment. I had to write off a year or more of work.

Where had I gone wrong?

The experimental problem was a good one. One reason for it being attractive was that so little experimental work had been done in this area. Probably other researchers had also become discouraged at the difficulties of instrumentation and data analysis. I had chosen an area that was relatively unexplored, for which there was not a large literature about the phenomenon itself, the instrumentation, or the techniques of data analysis.

- **Learning Number One:** Why not study something that other people have been studying for a while? You can learn from them and build on their experiences and findings. The instrumentation I used was unique. Literally, I had to build everything from the experimental chamber with its meter to the instruments which recorded and quantified the responses.

- **Learning Number Two:** Why not use instruments

or other techniques which have been developed,
tested and de-bugged by others? Look for things
that have stood the tests of time, be they techniques
of interviewing, personality tests, or sound meters.
The wheel has already been invented.

After several months of playing blues records and moping,
I got a job at Hamilton College in upstate New York. I soon
was doing a bit of consulting at a neighboring institution
which was in those days referred to a school for retarded
people. During coffee breaks the clinical psychologists
with whom I was consulting bemoaned the lack of basic
research on this very large population of institutionalized
people. Surely, they said, some things could be learned
which might well prove to be useful in assisting the population there. It was an invitation to work at a nearby site
with a population of people who were not only interesting
but accessible.

- *Learning Number Three*: Look for opportunities to
  work at a research site which offers a ready acceptance and available populations to study. In thinking over what research I could undertake, I recalled
  that one of my graduate school interests was the
  area of Discrimination. I use that word technically
  here to mean: human beings responding differently
  in the face of differing environments. We, as adults,
  call a dog " a dog" and a cat "a cat." Young children
  are not likely to have made that discrimination and
  can be heard summoning the dog with "Nice kitty"
  or "woofing" at the cat. One of the largest litera-
  tures in Human Psychology pertains to the development of discriminations. Well, I had learned Lesson
  Number One. So I began re-examination of that
  vast literature, knowing that I was travelling a road
  that many had traveled before.

I knew that I wanted to explore some basic processes in
human discrimination. I knew that I had a population
which had often been labelled "retarded" in part because of
difficulties in discrimination. More specifically, many
retarded children were said to have difficulties in delayed
discrimination or delayed recall. Say, that you show me
two pictures and then take them away. Now you ask me:
was the picture of the tree on the left or the right? I can
discriminate easily when the pictures are in front of me,

but I experience more difficulty as the time between presentation and recall is lengthened. The literature informed
me that some research had been done on delayed recall of
this sort. Experimental designs existed; some instrumentation was available; previous data were reported though not
in abundance. Lesson Two was in my head as I opted to
develop a study of delayed recall in retarded children.

In the pursuance of the literature and in setting up and
conducting the experiment, I learned another lesson.
Going way back in the history of the problem, I discovered
fascinating studies that both illuminated and amused.
One study was by a wonderful German woman who trained
a chimpanzee in delayed recall this way. She would show
him a coloured block and then drop it into a bag of blocks.
He would then labouriously go through the bag and select
the correct one. Having been burnt by previous failure,
working hard at my new job, and adjusting to a very different living environment (a small college high on a hill out in
the country with no New York City cabs available!) I can
remember the relief and joy when reading this wonderful
story and imagining this lady sitting in her kitchen carrying out the delayed study with her pet chimp!

- *Learning Number Four*: Enjoy every incident that
  you can as you wend your way through the thesis
  process. It need not be torture; you have not taken
  vows of unhappiness. Savor the fun parts.

Reinforcing this lesson was my work with the kids. What a
wonderful group they were. How they taught me new
meanings for the word "retarded!" One summer day a
group of these supposedly mentally incompetent kids,
labelled by one worker "pathetic," took me out to a little
fair on the hospital grounds. They insisted that, since I was
their guest, they should buy me ice cream and popcorn.
They counted out the money and checked their change! I
called over several of the teachers to watch the next epi-
sode, knowing that they would not believe my report. So I
learned from and enjoyed the contact with my so-called
experimental population.

The study was successful in terms of producing interesting data as well. I don't think that it advanced knowledge
of practice very much but it did give support to those who
sought more stimulating research activity at the institution.

Now I was at the point of writing it up. Another move: this time to the University of Michigan. Again, the new environment and new job slowed me down. Furthermore, as the distance in time and miles from Columbia increased, the support from the graduate faculty there naturally decreased. Some members of my old committee had retired or gone elsewhere. Luckily, I had a colleague and friend at Michigan, a fellow psychologist, Harlan Lane, who has gone on to do even more extraordinary things than helping me complete my dissertation. (Harlan has written importantly about hearing impaired people, sign language and so on. And he has become in the process a very visible and audible advocate for the deaf.)

Harlan used a hard line on me: we would meet two nights a week at the Center where I worked. We would work for one to two hours. At the outset I would tell him how many pages I would write; at the conclusion we would check on my work. (I guess that he read or wrote letters while I slaved away.) I did not always meet the criterion set. In fact an incidental learning was that I discovered how better to estimate the time it takes to write something. But slowly I ground out the manuscript. Oh, I should note that he instructed me to start with the materials that I thought would be easiest to write up. "Surely you know what you did. Why not start with the Methods and Procedure section?"

As the manuscript emerged (I am sure it was a sad looking thing at that time, but it got better with editing) it began to have a life of its own. His sacrificed evenings were no longer necessary and I finished it up.

- *Learning Number Five*: Maybe, as they say, you are born alone and you die alone; but you do not have to do a thesis alone. Once I got over the flush of embarrassment, or better, once fear and self-loathing had driven me to the arms of a friend, I could get to work in a collaborative environment.

So here I am today, not exactly a newly minted PhD, but remembering afresh the journey I took. Since then I have written many articles and chapters and conducted a lot of research which proves that not only life but also scholarly activity can continue after the oral defense. Another way to put this is that a thesis is one — just one — scholarly activity you are likely to undertake.

- ***Learning Number Six:*** All the world may be waiting for the sunrise or peace or prosperity, it is not breathlessly waiting for your thesis. The thesis should be done with some degree of perspective. Of course you are totally involved, as you may be at times with your children or your dog. But the thesis is only one brick in the path you are building.

- ***Learning Number Seven:*** Carrying out the thesis research and completing a successful defense is an opportunity to learn. The product is important, to be sure; but the process — the commitment, the development of expertise, the demonstration of your ability to stay with a most difficult task over a long time — is even more important if approached and carried out the right way.

I am not so sappy as to suggest the thesis experience was so grand and full of fun that I will undertake another thesis tomorrow. But if I had not done so I would have missed a great deal. And that is the final lesson.

You Don't Just Take a Thesis Journey, You Choose a Lifestyle

Mary Hookey

Thesis Title:

**Educational Consultation:
Reflections of Teachers and Resource Personnel**

Unpublished doctoral thesis,
University of Toronto, 1985.

What would you likely do if you had completed your
master's degree a year ago and missed the exchange of
ideas and the company of interesting, dedicated educators? You might take the same step that I did and enroll in
a doctoral program. When I think back to this decision, I
see that it was more than deciding to do a thesis; my thesis journey meant choosing a lifestyle.

Perhaps this choice was inevitable for me. I had spent
my first years in the world of work as a professional musi-
cian and chose to enter pre-service education later in life.
In those days, the entrance requirement for the elementary
pre-service program was a secondary school graduation
diploma. To upgrade my qualifications, I worked on my
Bachelor of Arts degree in the evenings after teaching and
in the summer. These long years of study were followed by
the Master of Education program. Despite the demands of
this work, the gains were always great. Meeting people
concerned with the same issues, and entering a silent
dialogue with the voices in library books continually
helped me deal with the complexities of teaching and
learning. When the master's program was completed, I
could always read a book; however, it was the people I
missed. There was also another incentive. Like some
women teachers, my life was defined by raising a family as
a single parent, teaching and studying.

The required residency of the doctoral program represented the first and only year beyond pre-service education in which I had the luxury of full-time study at university. Fifteen years after beginning my university program, the Etobicoke Board of Education granted me a leave of absence with pay for doctoral study. Their support and the support of my new husband gave me a secure personal start.

Getting a Handle on the Demands

I can remember asking many questions about just what doing doctoral work meant before I began the program. At that time, many students who started the program were dropping out without completing their theses, and I had no intention of joining that group. My future supervisor advised me to undertake the majority of my course work before enrolling as a full-time student and to begin the process of refining an area for research immediately. After two years, with all but the two required courses of the doctoral year left to complete, I was ready for concentrated work on the thesis. I will never forget how privileged I felt to have this opportunity as I travelled downtown to OISE on that first crisp September day of my sabbatical year. This memory always sustained me in the times when I wondered if I could meet the demands of the thesis process, particularly when I returned to full-time employment.

Using the Past to Frame the Future

I always think of my doctoral work as being grounded in the issues of professional collaboration and curriculum practice that I had faced daily. As a resource person I found many areas of education that needed study and attention. My work brought me into contact with teachers and students in a variety of classroom settings: single grades, multiple grades, classroom settings where students represented a wide range of backgrounds and abilities, and segregated educational programs for students identified as gifted, behaviorally challenged or autistic. Finding ways to negotiate an appropriate way to act as a resource in this wide range of situations was always stimulating work.

With the large variety of course offerings at OISE, we were able to design a program where issues of collaboration and curriculum could continually be explored. Some courses structured learning around issues that scholars and practitioners had already identified; others based the course on a process of critical reflection and self-initiated change. This balance of outside-in and inside-out helped me to locate my own practice in the context of a wider set of issues.

One of the most valuable activities at the beginning of the thesis process was the telling of my professional story. The yellowed pages of computer printouts in my proposal binder remind me that this was a demanding task, one that I returned to many times. This story was one of the interconnectedness of my experience with a whole range of students and colleagues, as well as speakers and writers on education. My belief in the importance of human relationships to professional learning and the values that I placed on negotiated interaction led me to select Hunt's (1987) theory to frame my research. Not only did I want to shed some light on the world of practice by examining it from a new perspective, I also wanted to determine what this perspective might mean to other educators.

Choosing what to collect as data and how to collect it was another challenge. I considered a case study, REP (Repertory Grid) tests and a variety of other approaches that would shed light on the problem I had selected. In the end, I decided on an interview study. In George Kelly's famous words, "If you want to know what someone thinks about something, ask them." The images of collaboration shared through these interviews provided a rich data base. The negotiations that I went through to locate and invite participation in the study were just as interesting, telling me as much about the context for collaboration as any pointed interview questions.

Although it has been more than a decade since I began my doctoral program, some aspects continue to influence my life work. One is the advice I received from my advisors. For example, there is one faded index card on my bulletin board at home with these words from David Hunt on it:

> As soon as you have done something, imagine that you had to make your case on what you know right now. What would you say? What would you focus on? How would you be compelling?

Dave made these remarks to me during one of our tape-recorded sessions when I was mesmerized by the minute detail and complexity of the interview data and not finding patterns in much of what I was hearing. In one short piece of advice, I had a frame for snapping out of this state and refocusing on the work of the thesis process.

"As soon as you have done something, . . ." Doing something" in a thesis is always action in the context of a problem. The problem statement proved to be the critical anchor, one that I could refer to even as I allowed myself digressions into fascinating but tangential territory.

"Imagine that you had to make your case on what you know right now. What would you say?" Making a case. Now that was a challenge. When I got bogged down in the complexity of my data, I couldn't imagine a bigger picture, let alone focus on the argument that I should make. One of the challenges of research methodology, which lets the issues and analysis emerge from ongoing data collection, is that you do not know in advance which particular case you will be making. You have to discover it, and that is hard work.

"What would you focus on?" This question prompted me to find new ways to make connections across the interviews. It was through my rough drawings of these connections that I discovered how much I could explain through graphic as well as verbal analysis.

"How would you be compelling?" This is one part that I am still working on. I admired fellow students who had taken English as a major in university and had become active and expressive writers. Describing the patterns in my data and explaining their meaning was demanding; however, the time I had spent typing each of the fifty interviews, had its rewards. I could hear the language ringing in my ears every time I thought about certain issues and tried to develop a point.

Making your case orally is just as important. It's a skill you will need both before, during and after the thesis defense. I had one challenging opportunity to state my case during a session for doctoral students at an annual ASCD (Association for Supervision and Curriculum Development) conference. Several students were presenting their research work in the area of instructional supervision. Their theses focused on the effects of supervision based on the match between the conceptual levels of the supervisors and teachers involved. In contrast, my work focused on the meaning of different ways that resource personnel might work with classroom teachers as a basis for a negotiated practice. Here I was, challenging their definition of assistance to teachers and questioning their theoretical base. It required the most compelling language that I could muster to make my case. Their response sharpened my appreciation between the mindset of those who "do to" others and those who "work with," a distinction now made frequently in the supervision literature.

Tips to Travellers

Curiosity can kill a cat and a marriage. A decade after I completed the thesis, Bob and I are still married. I look on that as an accomplishment. I don't know if anyone has done a study of marriage failure among doctoral candidates, but my personal observations tell me that the percentages must be high. Keeping in touch with the fact that the pressures you feel are also felt by a sensitive partner can help you pick up warning signals. People on the sidelines of the thesis process sometimes do not share their own concerns until it is too late.

If there's no choice, carry on. There will be times when you have too many demands on your time and no options. Certainly that is how I felt one weekend in the last year of my thesis work. My supervisor was leaving the country and had asked for the latest version of a chapter to take along on the trip. Since faculty time is precious, I had to get the work done. At the same time both my daughters were getting to the point where they were concerned about how little time we were devoting to each other. We needed to spend a few moments together, just the three of us, having a quiet dinner. There were no options. After our Saturday evening dinner, I headed down at 11:00 p.m. to the OISE computer room. I emerged at 6:45 A.M. Monday, chapter in hand. I did not realize how tired I was until I saw the sun come up in my rear view mirror as I travelled home across the Humber River Bridge.

One of my colleagues is now facing the same no-choice situations as she completes her thesis. Her husband gave her a large headline from the newspaper which reads, PEOPLE WHO STAY UP ALL NIGHT AT THE COMPUTER NEED PROFESSIONAL HELP. Maybe not. Maybe they are just doctoral students whose options have run out and who have made up their minds to make it through.

If you haven't got a question, don't start. Some days
the cafeteria seemed populated with bright, literate, ABD
(all-but-dissertation) doctoral candidates who found everything highly interesting but couldn't focus on a question or
concern that was really their own. No one expects you to
have THE QUESTION for your research on the first day of
your program, but you should have a passion about some
aspect of education and some emerging questions that
begin to focus your course work and research. My advice
is: Don't even start the doctoral program until you wake up
one morning and the excitement of the journey compels
you to begin and see it through. Make the grasp of your
own assumptions, motivation and understandings "Job
One" in the first months of your program. I found that
grounding my work in my own experience led me to more
than enough perplexing situations that would be worth my
time and effort.

The thesis is not an end; it's a beginning! Doing doctoral study is an occasion for sharpening your skills and
expanding your personal horizons. Keeping a focus on the
possibilities beyond the thesis defense can keep you motivated and help you to see opportunities as they present
themselves. I once asked a candidate what she was doing
at OISE, and her response was, "I'm preparing to be the
most current and knowledgeable person in my area when I
graduate." That comment sparked me to step out of the
complexity of data collection and analysis to reflect on the
place of the thesis in a balanced life.

If I Were a Guide

If I were a thesis supervisor, I would offer two suggestions,
one professional and one personal. Professionally, I would
encourage you to synthesize your own thoughts by writing
papers and dialoguing with scholars in your field at every
opportunity. Research conferences are excellent places to
sharpen your ideas and extend your thinking. Every doctoral student in education should go to the annual AERA
[American Educational Research Association] meeting. If
you have not made research conferences a favorite haunt,
now is the time to look for both regional and national
locations. Finding out how others are framing problems
and sharing research moves you quickly into the right
frame of mind for your own scholarly work.

Finally, and on a personal note, I would say, "Give your family this book." It seems only fair to help your significant others understand what they are getting into *before* you start. It also will remind them, as the years go by, that there is a light at the end of the tunnel. Since I have finished my thesis, I always read the dedications at the front of books. It is a gesture to all those who changed their own lives because they believed someone else could make a difference through study and writing.

In a very real sense, my story has not ended. My thesis is complete and sits on a shelf in the OISE library. I am reliving the process constantly with colleagues who are doctoral candidates. I think about the thesis work every time I read or design a study. That is maybe the clue to doing a thesis. It is not getting *through* the process; it's getting *into* a process that begins with a doctoral thesis. It's choosing a lifestyle.

Have You Travelled This Path Before?

David E. Hunt

Thesis Title:

Changes in Goal Object Preference as a Function of Expectancy for Social Reinforcement

Unpublished doctoral dissertation,
Ohio State University, 1953.

Thesis as Journey

Thesis as journey may refer to both the outer journey and the inner journey. Movement on your outer journey consists of meeting the formal requirements of forming a committee, writing a proposal, as well as carrying out the research activities — collecting material, analysing and interpreting material, and writing the chapters of the thesis. As you complete each requirement, activity, or chapter you move closer to your destination. You rarely travel in a straight line but the intermediate points such as proposal approval and collection of material are identifiable points on the map, and you will know when you have passed through one and are moving ahead.

Less clear but probably more important is your *inner* journey consisting of questions and issues such as: Is this trip really necessary?; mapping your inner resources, losing your way, dealing with roadblocks, and so on (Hunt, 1992, pp. 136-146). I would like to add to the questions you ask yourself on your inner journey: Have you travelled this path before?

Many travellers begin their doctoral thesis journey overwhelmed by the thought, "I've never done this before" which soon becomes, "How will I ever learn all the skills and knowledge needed to become a researcher in such a short time?" and may lead to, "I don't know anything about doing research; I'll never be able to do this." Such feelings are quite understandable since it is true for all of us when we begin that we have never done a doctoral thesis before. Most of us, however, have experience, skill, and knowledge in very *similar* activities; most of us have been researchers in our everyday inquiry; most of us have written proposals of one kind or another; almost everyone has informal experience with interviewing; and if you think about it, you probably have experience in pooling your impressions of another person, student, or client to form an interpretation. In short, you have travelled many of these paths before. So each time you confront a new portion of your outer journey, look inward to discover your earlier experiences with this activity and bring out your experienced knowledge and skills about this portion of your journey.

Cut through the mystique of the thesis by making it familiar through earlier experiences. One colleague suggested, "I thought about each chapter as a term paper. . . . I've written lots of term papers so it made writing the thesis less mysterious. When I had written five term papers, I was finished." Try it for yourself to discover whether this might be a way for you to demystify the daunting challenge of completing the thesis journey.

If you are an experienced practitioner planning to use interview and observation as methods, chances are you have travelled this path before. You may have conducted informal interviews with students, clients, and/or parents as well as participating as interviewee in job interview settings. Recall your own experiences to bring out your knowledge and skills in interviewing. Not that you will not need to improve your skill, but you are not starting from scratch. The same goes for observation. Most of us have a wealth of informal experience as observers of our students, clients, and colleagues. This will set the foundation for your using observation in your doctoral research.

Probably the most formidable and mystifying challenge in doctoral research is the analysis and interpretation. When you hear words like "heuristics," "hermeneutics," or "phenomenological" interpretation your reaction is likely, "I've certainly never travelled *this* path before," yet, this is probably not true. Take the example of interpreting material from an interview to form an impression of the interviewee as a person and to portray their beliefs and experiences. Such portrayal is challenging and may be a form of artistry, yet, it is not entirely foreign to most experienced professionals. Any time you attempt to formulate your impressions about one of your students or clients into a summary interpretation (whether formal or informal) in order to adapt to them in a more helpful way, you are engaging in meaning-making interpretation which is the cornerstone of qualitative interpretation in doctoral research.

My suggestions about how to be your own best theorist and how to be your own best researcher (Hunt, 1992) could be extended to how to be your own best epistemologist by unearthing your own unexpressed beliefs about how you know and what kind of knowledge counts for you. In all of these cases you explore your previous travels by recalling your previous experience and activities with the specific topic in order to tackle it as an experienced professional with implicit research skills and knowledge, not a beginner in the mysterious world of research.

A final comment about thesis as journey. Travellers all have their own specific version of their journey. One might view it as crossing the Rockies in a van, another as a canoe trip, still another as floating along in a balloon. I recommend that you try to evoke your own specific inner image of your thesis journey to make it as personally meaningful and practically valuable as possible.

Personal Images of Research and Your Topic

In addition to images of your doctoral thesis, you may evoke images of yourself as researcher as well as images of your specific research topic (Hunt, 1992, pp. 125-127). The image of the researcher in traditional research has often been the Scientist with a White Coat who was objectively observing and analysing the phenomenon under investigation. What is your image of yourself as a researcher? Some have seen themselves as making music with their participants, others as engaging in the cooperative attempt to solve a puzzle. Identifying your image will provide access to your underlying values and beliefs about the research process.

Some travellers also find it valuable to evoke an image of their research topic or the phenomenon they study. In addition, it may be valuable to evoke your participants' images of the phenomenon. For example, Brader Brathwaite (1988) began with her own image of teaching, that of a chalice, and then evoked images from her participants of how they imagined their teaching. Finally, she viewed their work together as an interplay between their images—for example, the participant's river flowing into her chalice.

Tips to Travellers

In my chapter on "Research as renewal" (Hunt, 1992) I offer numerous suggestions for moving along on the thesis journey. Here I will offer a few new ideas and repeat one or two which I believe are central.

1. Develop your intention statement

I suggest that travellers write their intention statement on a 3 x 5 card in 25 words or less, then show it to others for feedback. This activity sounds simple, but the evolution of an acceptable and comprehensive intention statement often takes considerable time. Once it has been developed, it serves as the center of the work. It helps you map out what you are investigating and, of equal importance, what you are not studying. As travellers work on their intention statement, they are encouraged to be alert to the intention statement of any research investigation they read about, theses and research articles. Doing so raises their awareness about the form and lexicon of the statement. For example, what is the difference between the verb "to explore" and "to demonstrate" in terms of research method and interpretation?

2. Follow your passion

I was amused recently by a suggestion in a how-to-do-it book on conducting a doctoral thesis in the social sciences, specifically psychology, that doctoral candidates should avoid selecting a topic in which they were emotionally involved, in other words be dispassionate when selecting the topic. This is the traditional wisdom. Now, in non-traditional approaches as I am writing about, it is the exact opposite: go with your passion.

Selecting a topic which is dear to your heart can be defended not only on the grounds that you are more likely to learn something valuable by doing so, but also on practical grounds. Many travellers who are experienced professionals must conduct the doctoral thesis when they return to their professional settings, and thus the thesis work must compete with their daily deadlines of their work. Yet the thesis has no external deadlines (except that after six years, you will be informed you are in lapsed candidacy) so travellers must develop their own deadlines. If you have not selected a topic which has personal importance to you, the chances of your completing it when you are back on the job are very slim indeed. Completion rates are low enough — usually around 50% — so arm yourself with a study that you want to complete. Follow your passion.

3. Tape recorders have many uses.
In addition to their serving as your basic instrument for collecting material, tape recorders are also important for recording other aspects of the thesis process such as, thesis committee meetings and meetings with supervisors. I began recommending the taping of supervisory sessions several years ago to those students who were less fluent in English, but since than I have come to recommend, and almost insist, that students I supervise tape our discussion meetings. Doing so frees them to listen in the meeting as well as to go back to the tape afterward and pick up aspects which might otherwise have been lost. It is even more important to tape record meetings of your thesis committee.

4. Begin at the beginning.
When it comes time to write your thesis, I strongly recommend that you begin writing the first chapter. This sounds so obvious that you may wonder why I bother to mention it. I have found, however, that many travellers go through the following sequence: complete proposal, begin collecting material, get interested in the analysis and want to write about it immediately, postponing the writing of the earlier chapters. Jumping into the middle of the thesis has many disadvantages. It prevents the flow of the work portraying the true sequence of activities which is very important for the reader. Also, postponing writing the earlier chapters often leads travellers to become bored with the introductory chapters because they have gone beyond them. They find it difficult to write and, when they do write, it is often lacking in zest and vitality. The thesis describes the process (or journey), and needs to depict that process as it happened, not a false record which shifts the sequence.

5. Your thesis is one of your most important relationships.

After completing her thesis several years ago, Sharon Bray discussed the process with doctoral students at an informal meeting. She began by noting that her relationship with her thesis had been intense and had made an impact on all of her other central relationships, especially with family. Therefore, my last suggestion is that you acknowledge this "new relationship" and discuss it with your nearest and dearest to attempt to negotiate an arrangement in which you can be there in all of your relationships as much as possible. This is easier said than done because family members rarely see an advantage for them from your "new relationship," viewing it rather as encroaching on your relationship with them. This is something that each traveller must negotiate personally, and will probably require continuing re-negotiation.

When I Was a Traveller

I began graduate work in the Fall of 1949 at Ohio State University, and I can still remember George Kelly's welcoming words to us: "We don't know what the Clinical Psychology of the future will look like, all we know is that it will be different, and we hope to prepare you for that future." As I recall my graduate school days, my most indelible memory is my participation in research teams. George Kelly and Jules Rotter were both working on major books which they hoped would provide a theoretical base for the new Science of Clinical Psychology. Kelly and Rotter each met with their students weekly in non-credit research teams' meetings to discuss theoretical issues, to reflect on a new chapter from their books, and most often to consider the thesis work of students on their teams.

Having worked with Kelly on my master's thesis, I wanted the best of both worlds so I joined Rotter's team for my doctoral thesis. As students, we were probably not aware at the time of the enormous value of learning from each other. In the research team discussions we learned from peers who were further along in the thesis process and we spent many hours with one another working on our doctoral thesis plans. Part of the value of those research teams can be realized in thesis support groups, but I think that the best possible arrangement is for faculty members to meet regularly with their students. Following my own advice, I have done so intermittently over the years, but wish I had done it more frequently. There is something about meeting with others who are at different stages in their journey yet who have common destinations which can be very powerful. It also acknowledges how much travellers learn from one another.

My next specific memory is New Year's Eve, 1952 where we toasted to "PhD in '53," or at least some of us did. The next morning, New Year's Day, believe it or not, I rose and went out to the Bureau of Juvenile Research (where I had completed my one-year internship the year before) to pilot my thesis methodology with juveniles who were in residence there. As you see at the beginning of my comments, my thesis title was appropriately incomprehensible. The dejargonized description was: how elementary age boys change their interest in playing with a toy when they have experienced adult approval for playing with it.

I also remember that shortly thereafter, my supervisor told me that it was time to collect my data so I set about arranging schools in which I could run my subjects. Things were very different forty years ago, and I was a part of that zeitgeist which believed that a new and scientifically based clinical psychology would be the answer to the nation's mental health problems. Put another way, it would have been difficult if not impossible to begin with myself in those days, even if I had chosen to work with George Kelly's theory of personal constructs.

It is interesting to speculate about what future researchers in 2033 will think of our work today. I am glad for my experience as a traveller. It gave me a valuable foundation. Perhaps the main point is that it took me so long to realize that a great deal of what I learned came from my peers. Travelling together makes the journey more enjoyable and meaningful.

The Journey Continues: From Traveller to Guide

Solveiga Miezitis

Thesis Title:

An Exploratory Study of Divergent Production in Preschoolers

Unpublished doctoral thesis,
University of Toronto, 1968.

My own journey began in 1958 with my master's thesis. I was enrolled in the Psychology Department at the University of Toronto and had planned a longitudinal study of the effects of group therapy on the attitudes of alcoholics towards self and significant others using the Semantic Differential. I had pretested sixty subjects, as we called our research participants back in those days, but only three came back for the post-test six months later. To make things worse, my advisor made himself scarce and was not available for further comment. As far as he was concerned, the study was a dismal failure and his supervisory commitment had expired. After the initial shock and a brief period of disbelief and bewilderment, I moved on to another research idea and another supervisor. This time I opted for a quick experimental study of the effect of positive and negative verbal reinforcement on the shaping of acquiescent verbal responses among nursing students. The study was completed and written up in record time of one month just in time for my June 1959 graduation deadline. Later on I understood that the information that I had collected on my sixty alcoholics would have sufficed for several master's theses. What I had lacked was insight and direction.

I learned several useful lessons from this experience for my future role as a guide. First, never to abandon a student who ran into trouble; second, to be careful about suggesting longitudinal studies with unstable populations over whom one has no direct control; third, that there is more than one way to approach a problem and that one's thesis need not be condemned to failure by rigid adherence to one's initial hypothesis. We are deluded by the articles published in academic journals that the research journey inevitably follows a clear and predictable linear path from its inception to its logical conclusion. What really happens in the course of many "unsuccessful" or aborted studies would fill twice as many journals on false starts and negative findings, and much could be learned from the real stories that researchers seldom get a chance to tell.

The drama of my PhD thesis revolved first around finding a worthwhile topic and then, finding a supervisor willing to support me on my road to discovery. Being persevering by nature, I was not ready to give up on the Semantic Differential after my fiasco with the master's thesis. Naively I thought that a viable thesis topic would emerge from diligently reading books and journal articles on Osgood's psycholinguistic theory. I wasted an entire summer in the library stacks among dusty volumes and emerged pale and empty handed. Instead of picking up on my previous experience with the Semantic Differential, I turned to theory believing this to be the best source for generating hypotheses that would lead to a significant contribution to science. The fantasy of making a great scientific discovery and writing the definitive magnum opus can be a major pitfall impeding progress on the thesis path.

Feeling very stressed, I picked up a new book on stress by Janis and Hovland and became caught up with the notion of replicating some of their work on adults with young children. By now I was a part-time instructor at the Institute of Child Study and could access children for research purposes. Filled with excitement, I immediately wrote a preliminary proposal and took it to one of the few professors who was interested in personality theory and actually talked about motivated action instead of stimuli and responses mediated through a black box. I was chagrined to have my hopes dashed. Apparently you could not study stress in children because it could not be pre-

cisely measured in human subjects and I was advised to
work with pigeons instead.

The vogue at the time was to operationalize stress levels
by subjecting pigeons to white noise. I was appalled at the
prospect of "running pigeons," birds which I generally
dislike, after having already spent months "running white
rats" through mazes for my third year learning course
project. The memories of that experience included having
my finger bitten by my furry white subjects and being sent
off for painful tetanus shots by my supervisor Professor
Tulving, who also deducted 10% from my final mark for
having naively suggested that my findings might have
some implications for humans. I lost all interest in animal
studies and was cured from anthropomorphizing forever.
Obviously "running pigeons" was not going to tell me anything about stress in humans and I decided to drop the
topic.

I was angry and discouraged and decided to drop out of
the Psychology Department after having completed all the
requirements, including foreign language exams in French
and German, the major doctoral challenge back in those
days when a PhD graduate still carried an aura of the well
educated Renaissance man. Women, except for a very few
eminent exceptions, did not figure very prominently in the
lofty circles of academia. A few weeks after my desertion,
the department chair hauled me in for a much feared
discussion about the dire consequences of dropping out. I
told him my tale of woe but he did not have any redeeming
suggestions to make. Operationalizing one's variables was
the name of the game during the ascendency of behavior-
ism. The once famous humanists who established the
name of Psychology at the University of Toronto, had been
replaced with a new breed of hard nosed experimentalists
who heralded in a new era of the little rg's little rf's and
other equally famous constructs that have since sunk into
oblivion.

Meanwhile, I was offered a full-time research and teaching position at the Institute of Child Study (ICS) by its
founder and director Bill Blatz , who was about to retire. I
decided to accept the job despite the minimal wage which
sufficed the independently wealthy staff who prevailed at
ICS at that time. My main motivation for joining the faculty had to do with the fact that it was embarking on a
new longitudinal study and the ideas of junior faculty were

solicited and well received. I had just come across a new book by Getzels and Jackson entitled *Creativity and Intelligence* and was once more caught up with a research idea. The longitudinal study provided the perfect opportunity to include measures of divergent thinking along with other intellectual measures for four-year-olds. I developed an experimental measure and became engrossed in the project. My PhD aspirations had not entirely vanished but I held no hope of finding a sympathetic advisor for my project.

In the meantime, my husband, an aeronautical engineer out of work because of the closing of the aeronautical industry in Toronto, was retraining at the Ontario College of Education to become a math and physics teacher. I picked up his bulletin by chance and discovered that there was a PhD program listed under Educational Theory. I made an appointment with the associate dean, Clifford Pitt, who was a psychologist and art buff, to discuss the possibility of transfer into their PhD program. He was very interested in my divergent thinking project and welcomed me into their program with an added year of residence to make up for my lack of education background. This turned out to be a very positive educational experience for me for several reasons. First, I was treated like a respectable human being with interesting research ideas; second, I was the first person in ten years to enrol in their PhD program and this gave me a special status and the right to make choices that met my educational needs best at the time; third, I was completely absorbed in my newly found interest in creativity and was able to negotiate my course assignments within this area of study; fourth, I had a stronger academic background than most of the EdD students there and enjoyed the opportunity to excel in adapting my psychology expertise to education; fifth, and most important, I presented my thesis proposal for a longitudinal study of divergent thinking in preschoolers and it was accepted and deemed interesting and potentially valuable to education.

Finally I had an approved thesis topic and my research was already under way; however, I did not have anyone who was specializing in this area to direct my study. Being a self-initiating, independent type, I did not consider it a problem at the time. All went well until it was time for analysing the data and I began to flounder. I did not have anyone to turn to and I began to doubt whether I really had a thesis. I badly needed guidance, from someone who understood what I was trying to do. I travelled to Atlanta, Georgia to visit the children's creativity guru Paul Torrance and had a nice visit, but no real feedback about my work. I was on the verge of giving up when luckily, at the AERA conference in Los Angeles, I was introduced by a mutual friend to Sister Rose Amata McCartin, a wonderful colleague, who had just completed a doctoral thesis on divergent thinking in six year olds, and had identified a verbal fluency factor. She understood my topic and empathized with my problem with the thesis. The hour which I spent in my hotel room talking to Sister Rose provided the validation and the feedback which I needed to renew my faith in the worth of my project and set me on a new path for analysing my data using factor analysis. Peer support and external validation can be invaluable at critical times to enable students to get over thesis blocks and dispel the debilitating attacks of self- doubt. I felt I was back on track and I was able to seek out the statistical advice which I needed to complete the analysis.

I handed in the first draft of my thesis three days before the birth of my second child. I learned from this experience that personal deadlines can be very energizing and can motivate students to accomplish incredible feats towards the completion of their theses. Meanwhile OCE had become part of the newly formed Ontario Institute for Studies in Education and I had my own formal thesis committee, including an expert in my area. This was the first time that the new committee had laid eyes on my thesis. Revisions were required and I experienced yet another wave of doubts about the outcome of my thesis journey. After spending an inordinate amount of time in completing the first draft, students often feel defeated when their product is found wanting. It took me another six months to complete the additional stepwise regression analyses in the days of hand wired computer programming and to prepare the bound copy for the oral defense. In those days students went to their orals with bound copies of their thesis which added an undue weight of finality to this event.

As the date of the senate orals approached, my perfectionist tendencies and self-doubts blossomed forth like cactus flowers after the first spring rain in the Arizona desert. I was reading up on methodological issues and analysing all the pros and cons of various factor analytic approaches in preparation for potential weaknesses in my oral defense; however, the major attack on my thesis came on a completely different and totally unexpected front. The internal University of Toronto examiner from my former department had announced to the chair of my thesis committee her intention to fail me at the senate orals on the grounds that I had used The House Test, a piece of equipment designed by a colleague at the Institute of Child Study as part of the procedure in setting up the divergent thinking task which I had designed for my thesis. The children were asked to complete a puzzle forming a house which they then had to decorate with various objects made from pieces of felt and tell about them. The internal examiner was essentially charging me with plagiarism. I was stunned by this development. It made no sense but it was obvious that she was out to get me.

My committee interpreted her response as a power move since I was to be the first graduate of the newly formed Department of Applied Psychology at OISE. We were perceived as unwanted competition that the Psychology Department had been trying to block. My committee carried out well-organized defensive tactics which included a review and ranking of all the doctoral theses completed by students at the Psychology Department during the past ten years in order to establish a standard for the evaluation of my thesis and its relative merits on various criteria. My all male committee was pleased that my thesis stood up well to the test and was merrily gearing up for what they perceived to be just another round in their prolonged battle with the Psychology Department.

In the midst of all this furor my committee had completely forgotten that I had never had a meeting with them on my thesis and that I did not have any idea of what the defense might involve. I felt extremely anxious and was not looking forward to the humiliation of the impending attack from the internal examiner. Needless to say I did not have the mind set for a brilliant defense and I am still amazed at the degree of memory impairment and outright confusion which I experienced during my orals. I could not remember any of my well-grounded arguments related to my choice of factor analyses and felt even more upset about my state of confusion as I tried to answer the perfectly reasonable questions of my supportive committee than about the internal examiner's irrational attack. I was impressed with the overwhelming effects of anxiety elicited by this final rite of passage and the need to provide students with the opportunity for desensitization at a departmental oral.

After the oral the first committee member to congratulate me said "You have earned your PhD, but that woman does not deserve to have hers." It was clear to me that she had cast a NO vote despite my explanation. I felt relief but no joy over my hard earned PhD. This was not cause for a celebration. The evidence of political in-fighting during my oral defense left me feeling cynical and very diffident about the fairness of the process.   My somewhat unusual, yet very painful experience stood in the way of my embarking on doctoral thesis supervision for many years to come, although I was greatly enjoying thesis work with my master's students. It is also ironic that to this day I have not published my doctoral study identifying verbal and non-verbal divergent thinking factors in children as young as four, although to my knowledge these findings have not been replicated by anyone else.

What did I learn from my own passage through the thesis labyrinth for my own future role as a guide? First, I was very aware of the complexity of the entire process and the need for support and encouragement at its different stages. Secondly, due to my own rather traumatic experiences, I became very sensitized to the fact that the guide's own thesis journey is likely to impinge on feelings and expectations in relation to his or her students. Since the process tends to be difficult because it can evoke deep-seated emotional issues which challenge the supervisor-advisee relationship at various stages, one needs to carefully consider which students one is most likely to be able to guide through the journey successfully. The fact that supervisors have very different rates of success in graduating their doctoral candidates attests to the fact that there may be more than academic issues involved.

Supervisors and supervisees attract one another for different reasons and some of these may not always lead to a successful union. One colleague, for example, had inordinately high standards for himself that interfered with his own success in research and publishing, and he frequently attracted students with a perfectionist bent. Needless to say, most of his students took years to complete, if at all, and the work they turned out often missed the mark by being over-focused on detail. This man completed his own PhD at a renowned university and had undergone very harsh treatment by his committee during his own journey. Another colleague, an independent minded, highly innovative and prolific academic, is open to a wide variety of ideas, but some of his students take an inordinately long time to complete their theses because they undertake overly ambitious projects. Another colleague is reluctant to insist on changes before the final orals but sides with external critics at the senate oral. This kind of situation leads to embarrassment for all involved. There are also impulsive, highly demanding colleagues who ask their students to rewrite proposals several times and sometimes, after all the furor and anxiety, the original version is accepted. These kinds of people can also become very ego-involved in forcing their own point of view and prevent students from finishing until they comply with their requests. If the student is stubborn, then very lengthy power fights can ensue. It makes one wonder how many students never graduate because of such impasses. Not only is the student-supervisor match important but so is the chemistry of the thesis committee. An awareness of the politics of the thesis process can be a critical factor in the length of time it takes and, ultimately, the difference between success or failure of some thesis journeys.

Over the years I have discovered my own strengths and limitations as a thesis guide. My major strength is my perseverance and commitment to guide candidates to a successful finish. My track record as a supervisor shows very few dropouts in an institution that has a fairly high rate of non-completion of doctoral theses. However, with some students the process takes too long, which suggests that I still have a lot to learn about the business of effective guiding. When I take on a doctoral student, I do so with the expectation that he or she will successfully complete the thesis under my guidance. Not being particularly selective about my master's students and having run into some difficult situations which could be fatal in a doctoral thesis relationship, I have learned a fair bit about myself and the ingredients that make for a good match.

I work well with students who show intellectual curiosity and a reasonable degree of independence and are willing to

undertake the thesis project as a challenge to their professional and personal growth. I find it much harder to work
with students who are overly dependent and compliant, or
who do not have any sense of commitment to what they
want for themselves out of this experience. These are the
students who are more concerned about playing by the
rules than about the substance of their thesis project. I
recognize that there is a strong element of personal identification involved and that a critical ingredient in the match
are shared values and expectations. The problem with
independent minded people is that they can be quite stubborn and a few candidates have shown extreme resistance
to requests for changes. In one instance, after a year of
unproductive struggle, I allowed the final battle to be
played out between the candidate and the external examiner, who was finally able to get the point across. In another difficult case, the student persisted for three years in
presenting her own story instead of elaborating on the
thesis work itself. To my great surprise, I just received an
entirely different third draft which incorporated all of my
previous suggestions, along with a note of apology and an
acknowledgment of our previous struggle as part of her
own personal growth process.

   As I look back on my own journey and that of my doctoral students, I recognize that there is a strong connection between the two and that in some cases, elements of
my own journey continue to be played out in the process.
During the writing of this chapter, I have been reminded
once more how important it is to begin with an awareness
of ourselves in all human interactions, particularly ones
as complex and fraught with potential pitfalls as the thesis
traveller-guide relationship.

Postscript

In order to remain true to my own story, I refrained from
reading any other material on thesis writing. As soon as I
was finished, I read Rennie and Brewer's (1987) paper on
thesis blocking. The paper is based on interviews with
doctoral candidates classified as blockers and non-block-
ers. To my surprise most of the major issues which
emerged in my own narrative were also discussed in their
research report. Such factors as dependence-independ-
ence, structuring the task in terms of personal meaning,
political expertise, and time management were the major

variables that seemed to make the difference. In addition to these, the student-supervisor match, the chemistry of the thesis committee, and the potential impact of the guide's own experiences, had emerged from my recollections as important factors which can also contribute to the speed and ultimate success of the traveller's thesis journey.

Never Give Up

Donald Musella

Thesis Title:

Open- and Close-mindedness as Related to the Rating of Teachers by Administrators: Implications for Administrative Theory Based on Superordinate-Subordinate Role Relationships

Unpublished doctoral dissertation, State University of New York at Albany, 1965.

Reflections of a Supervisor: Some Lessons for Others

Lesson One: Know Your Supervisor
Translated to mean know the supervisor's philosophy and preferred style of supervision, as well as academic work and track record with respect to quality feedback and turn-around time (dependability) with written submissions.

Who or What is a Supervisor? Obviously, the term supervisor projects a variety of images — classroom teacher, lion tamer, an expert with an all-knowing ego, a loving parent, life guard, a colleague. Perhaps the role is an everchanging one and all of the above are realistic images when played out through the behaviors of the university thesis supervisor. I play various roles depending on the student, the circumstances and the nature of the interactions among the various players — student, colleagues on the committee, and self. Having said that, I have come to realize that two rather differing roles emerge which reflect conflicting value positions.

Many of my colleagues see the supervision role as a

supportive one, which, when operationalized, results in psychological counselling behavior. They are proactive in attempting to foster self-esteem and in providing motivation strategies directed to encourage and induce the student to complete the thesis. I also see my role as supportive, but behave in quite different ways. My objective is to create a high degree of self reliance. Hence, the development and completion of the thesis rests solely on the student and calls for substantial self-initiated behavior. For example, some of my recurring lines: "If you never give me something to read, you will never hear from me; on the other hand, if you give me something to read, you will have a critical response within two days." "My door is almost always open; however, don't expect me to initiate a discussion about your thesis." "If you don't care about finishing the thesis, why should I?" Does this sound rather cruel? Perhaps it does for those students who are looking for nurturing; however, I believe I am working with adults who aspire to leadership positions. The thesis is but another opportunity to practice leadership skills. Completion of the thesis should be enough of an incentive to motivate the student.

Another important supervisory behavior is early turnaround time. I believe that immediate feedback is more important and useful than delayed feedback. We all know the example of the professor who has an average turnaround time of four to six weeks. Using the business metaphor, this seems to me to be a waste of money and time for the student. A thesis resting on the supervisor's desk increases the cost-benefit ratio in terms of financial, psychological, and intellectual loss: financial because the delay does not produce anything and, conversely, leads to increased costs for the student; psychological because it leads to frustration and emotional pain for the student who is directly dependent on the behavior (mercy) of the supervisor; intellectual because delayed feedback leads to a longer start-up period and causes an extended period of re-learning on the part of both the supervisor and the student.

Lesson Two: Develop a Strategy for Initiating a Thesis

Translated to mean: (1) keep the initial ideas relatively simple and easy to communicate and understand; and (2) reduce the process to two steps: asking questions and deciding on how to get the answers. At this stage avoid cluttering the written material with a lot of "camouflage"; use the technique of "bottom-lining."

What is a Thesis? Although this question most often is not worded this way, I find that many students want me to answer this question. See if you recognize some of these questions and statements (which are really questions) seeking approval.

> How does one start to "find" a thesis?
>
> Do I have to know a lot of statistics?
>
> I want to avoid a number thesis and want to use "real" data?
>
> How long should a thesis be?
>
> I want to do something practical.
>
> I'd like to do something on school-based management; my superintendent is going to introduce this into our system next year.
>
> I want to do a theoretical study but the professors I've talked to want me to collect data.

One of my standard first-step suggestions to students is to pick one or two areas of interest, develop a list of questions, the answers of which will solve one or more problems in these areas, and meet with me for a discussion. At the same time the student is advised to search the literature and thesis references to identify what others have written in these areas. The next step is the formulation of a draft proposal which includes one or more questions and procedures for obtaining answers to these questions.

Lesson Three: Practice Good Time Management Skills

This is more than being more efficient in time spent on tasks. It means adopting a philosophy of focusing on major high priority goals and setting aside quality time to complete the required tasks.

What Gets in the Way? The delay in thesis completion continues to be seen as a problem in various accountability reviews of university programs. Why do students take so long to complete theses? The concern goes beyond increasing efficiency in universities. To me it is a reflection on the negative cultural impact universities can have on students. Some of the answers I have experienced to the question of why the delay in completion might serve to remind us that delays can be intentional as well as unintended. Consequently, I leave it to the student to judge the value of the delay.

Given a certain amount of overlap, I have listed some reasons given to me by students for a delay in thesis completion:

- my present job takes most of my time;
- personal family problems have overwhelmed me, physically and emotionally;
- I've been reading everything I can find on the topic;
- my computer was down;
- I need to complete all my courses before I can even think about a thesis;
- I've been spending all my time preparing for the comprehensive examinations;
- my supervisor has not returned my last draft;
- it was too late to collect data in schools by the time I was ready;
- I've collected so much data I'm having a difficult time in organizing the material;
- I needed this holiday after such a heavy year;
- I need to run my data through again (fourth time) to see what else I can find;
- my mother has been ill;
- you never call me to see how I'm doing;
- I took on a new position and haven't had time to get re-organized;
- I've decided that other activities have a higher priority;
- I can't seem to focus on a thesis topic.

Some events in our lives are beyond our control. In my experience these events account for a small part of the reason for delays in completing the thesis. The lack of skills and knowledge also play a very minor part in causing delays. The main reason is simply that the student has placed thesis activity at a low priority in terms of time and interest. We all have the same amount of time. We usually can chose what to do with some, if not most, of our allotted time.

When I was a Traveller

I completed my doctoral thesis twenty-seven years ago. I was told that I completed the thesis in record time. What factors lead to the early completion? I offer some reflections on these pleasant yet frustrating times.

I had completed a master's thesis several years earlier. The experience of conducting research and writing the thesis was not entirely new to me. A super-critical supervisor at the master's level changed my expectations thus making it easier for me to take on the challenge of what was to follow in doing the doctoral thesis.

Secondly, my administrative experience was such that a normal day meant working on several tasks at the same time and practicing time control on task in order to meet the various deadlines. Adding the thesis to my list of activities did not cause exceptional changes in my conditions of work.

Being goal-directed and having a high level of work ethic values also were key factors. This is evidenced by the fact that I completed my thesis during the first year of a new administrative position. I had to resort to one of the key time management principles, i.e., working each day on the high priority items, which for me was starting each day early in the morning with the thesis prior to going to work.

The one single thought that motivated me during my doctoral studies was "if they can do it, so can I." The "they" in this case were the professors I had in graduate school. The one other thought that accompanied this one was "I can't afford (literally) to take much time with the thesis." With a family and little money and no position during residence time, the cost seemed too high to "waste" this time in my life.

Reflecting on my experience says much about me. I never felt the need to have the supervisor do anything but critique my work. Perhaps now as a supervisor I have difficulty nurturing students who seem to me to lack the motivation to move through to completion, because I expect them to be like me. My error, however, is generalizing from a case of one. I need to move to greater understanding of those who come to the doctoral program with different experiences, style and values from mine.

Lesson Four: Never Give Up

This reminds me of two students I had written off because I had not heard from them for over two years. Within the same week I received complete drafts of the thesis from each of them. A pleasant surprise — two excellent theses needing little change after years of no contact. They, independently, had decided not to give up and had avoided me until they had something to show. You never know how wrong your predictions can be when dealing with others. That is the final lesson.

Exploring the Country is Not Climbing a Ladder

Margaret (Peggy) Patterson

Thesis Title:

A Study of the Externship Experiences of Veterinary Students

Unpublished doctoral thesis,
University of Toronto, 1991.

> *Understanding a form of knowledge is far more like coming to know a country than climbing a ladder*
> (Hirst, 1965).

The most effective way of describing my doctoral thesis journey is to use the metaphor that helped to guide my thinking during the research process — the image of "coming to know a country." This metaphor captures both the scale of the thesis journey and the scope of the learning — learning about the "country" of the thesis itself, understanding the rules and customs, learning the language, choosing travel companions, choosing an itinerary, and then embarking on the journey.

The journey that I undertook for my doctoral research, through interviewing students before, during and after their clinical practicum, was an exploration and description of the clinical apprenticeship experience that veterinary students acquire in their Externship placement at the Ontario Veterinary College.

This exploration revealed that the Externship proved to be an extensive source of learning and professional socialization for the participants. Besides providing an opportunity for integrating their clinical and theoretical knowledge, the Externship experience highlighted the importance of opportunities to learn about human relations, to make the transition to practice, to increase clinical skill and to increase participants' confidence in their own knowledge. The research procedure of reflecting on their own experiences and using this reflection as a source of learning was also highly valued by the participants.

The **country** of the thesis that I had entered was truly foreign to me. I had no idea of what a doctoral thesis was! So, as part of a doctoral course, as well as on my own, I read dozens and dozens of doctoral theses in an attempt to understand the "territory." I puzzled through many questions: How long is a doctoral thesis? How formal is a doctoral thesis? What types of research constitute doctoral research? How many "subjects" does one need in a doctoral study? What is the format of a doctoral thesis? How similar are thesis proposals to the final product?

Thus, by exploring the written theses, and discussing doctoral research process-features with several recent graduates, I began to get an image of the physical relief of the country that I was now visiting.

The second task associated with journeying in this foreign country was to **understand the rules and customs** to be followed by visitors. Although I understood that the research process itself was complicated, I had no idea that there were so many guidelines, forms, ethical reviews, and deadlines that a doctoral student must follow. It was like trying to understand the "immigration requirements" for entering a new country — they were written in a very formal way, and needed translation by a native speaker! The opportunity to discuss my concerns with my supervisor and other doctoral students helped me to understand these customs and to begin to understand that any new journey had its own fair share of paper work.

In addition to learning about the rules and customs, one of the other important tasks when entering thesis country was to **choose my travel companions**. Specifically, it meant determining who my thesis committee would be, in consultation with my supervisor. This task required that I understand a lot about my topic and about the research process itself, and could therefore only take place once I had a good idea of the research that I wanted to do. I invited committee members to join me who brought their own strengths to the process — both in terms of content expertise and in terms of the personal resources they brought to the "journey" of the research. One brought an understanding of the terrain of higher education, one brought an understanding of research methodology, and my supervisor brought a wealth of experience both in the content of experiential learning and in the learning process itself — he knew the thesis journey extremely well and was agile in climbing up and down the slopes and navigating the rivers with me, the novice traveller.

The most challenging aspect of the thesis journey, however, was determining the **itinerary** for my journey. My thesis topic began with an idea that emerged through discussions in a doctoral course. We were required to develop a short intention statement of where we wanted to go on our thesis journeys and to revise and transform this statement over a 12 to 13 week period. This exercise served as the opportunity I needed to sharpen the focus of what I wanted to do, and where I wanted to go on my journey.

Again, as part of the course, I found that by being interviewed by a fellow classmate about my topic, and by having the opportunity to explore my own experience with research and to interview possible participants, I became better informed about the scale of the journey that I wanted to undertake. I think the most important thing I learned from this process was that I could not research all of thesis country, but instead I needed to sharpen my focus into one "province" or area and to define this area clearly.

It was at this topic selection/proposal writing phase that I experienced my first crisis of confidence. Through a review of completed theses, through discussions with people who had completed their thesis journeys, and through discussions with my supervisor, I began to internalize the scale of the task that I was about to undertake. I also began to reflect on my views and opinions of those who had completed their doctoral theses... I held them in very high esteem. The thought, that I was embarking on a journey that would take me to the same place as they were, challenged my own confidence. I began to feel that I was not up to the task, I was fraudulent. Because of the public nature of the thesis process and because of the way in which it is evaluated, both through internal and external appraisers, I questioned my own competence and "right" to join this esteemed group. This concept of "feeling like a fraud" has been explored in detail by McIntosh (1985, 1989). These feelings were very overwhelming and delayed my proposal writing process.

As I thought about my guiding quote: "Understanding a form of knowledge is far more like coming to know a country than climbing a ladder," I decided to embark on a thesis process quite intentionally on a step-by-step process, by completing one task at a time. Although the scale of the entire task was overwhelming, I could focus on the next step ahead of me. So, like a traveller inching along a narrow ledge overlooking a deep cavern, I could not look over the edge, or around the corner, but could put one foot in front of the other and do one thesis task at a time. Although, I was able, in the end, to make progress using this strategy, the numbers of times that I "felt like a fraud" were numerous and varied.

Once I had finally committed to my topic/journey, the Externship experience of veterinary students, the focus of my attention began to shift from my own journey to that of the participants in my study. I was fortunate in getting significant cooperation from the Ontario Veterinary College, both in terms of access to participants and encouragement to embark on the journey, and the participants themselves were both willing and able to help me learn what I wanted to learn.

What I was unprepared for was how personally connected I became to the participants and their journeys. This may have been emphasized by the fact that I was a woman and within the veterinary school, although 70 per cent of the students are women, there are relatively few role models for them. Therefore, women veterinary students were looking for role models from whom to learn veterinary skills, but also women role models who could help them to understand how one would combine the personal and professional aspects of one's life. Although I could not tell them what to do, through sharing their experiences and through later follow-ups, they were able to have this aspect of their experience both heard and valued. I also felt privileged to be invited to the graduation of these students, to see how the Externship had in fact contributed to their education.

When I embarked on the thesis journey, I had the belief that the most difficult and time-consuming part of the thesis process was the data collection phase. I was wrong.

The thesis process is much more like building a house where significant time is spent drawing up the initial plan, and putting up the exterior walls and roof, and yet, almost two-thirds of the work remains once the house looks complete. So it was with my thesis. The collection of the research data from the participants was like having the house "framed in" — there was a lot of finishing carpentry to be done!

The process that I had undertaken involved my completing the transcriptions of all the tapes, summarizing my findings and then analysing them. This task required large blocks of uninterrupted time, a real challenge for me since I was working full-time during the entire thesis journey. Many evenings, weekends, and holidays later, however, I emerged with my collected understandings about the learning outcomes from the Externship experience. The "journey" of my thesis revealed many high points and "peak experiences," some challenging terrain, some major pitfalls, and some real insights into "the natives" of this country. My respect for students, for practitioners, and for veterinary clinical education was both increased and enhanced through my research process. I truly felt privileged to have had an opportunity to share this journey with these expert guides.

Once again in the research process I had a crisis of confidence. The thesis journey requires that one step back from the research to discuss it and to assess the implications of the results. Since I had been so close to this research for so long, I found this task challenging, and, in fact, the first draft of my discussion was merely a reworking of my Results section! After numerous attempts at discussion, I decided to change my technique. The data analysis had required an extensive use of visual learning; however, the actual research process was an interview process, focused on auditory learning. I found that learning from an auditory mode, a mode that is familiar to students and to me, proved to be an effective way to overcome this "block." I tape-recorded myself reading the results, and then I listened to the tape many, many times, until, through being able to distance myself from the direct experience, I was able to see patterns, themes, and important points that I could not see when they were in written form. Changing my learning style was essential at this stage in the journey. Interestingly, this could correspond to learning a new language for travel in a foreign country. One can only learn so much from the written word and, sometimes, one needs to begin to listen to how it is spoken to be able to pick up the subtleties of meaning and inflection that come from the language, rather than focusing on the precision and rigidity of the written word. Words need contexts and these contexts also have patterns of meaning which emerge when one hears several of them together. This technique helped me to overcome the impasse and I was finally able to complete the writing of my thesis.

I had planned the journey, and now I had completed the journey. What remained was summarizing my journey for my travelling companions and completing my thesis defense. One interesting aspect of a thesis journey is just how personal the process becomes. I found that during the data analysis and discussion phases of my thesis, I became totally absorbed in the thesis and had great difficulty focusing on such necessary things as my day-to-day work, my family, and personal responsibilities. The thesis became my journey and with the completion of the thesis, I needed to re-enter the rest of my world.

In discussions with my thesis committee and travel companions, I was pleased that they were able to both value and respect the journey that I had been on, and also provide me with some useful suggestions about how to improve the descriptions of my findings for others who might want to follow me into "the country" of my thesis. In addition, the thesis defense process, although challenging, was a wonderful opportunity to share both the excitement and the experience of my research process with the Examination Committee. Far from being a "hurdle" to cross on the way out of thesis country, I now found myself transformed into an individual who no longer felt fraudulent, a fellow traveller who had the opportunity to share her adventures in the country of the Externship with fellow colleagues who were also interested in this experience.

Finally, although the thesis process was complete, my own journey was not. Just as a visitor to a new country can leave with memories, souvenirs, and experiences that become part of the fabric of their lives, so my research journey into the Externship experience and through doctoral thesis country was equally transforming. I was not the same person who began the journey many years before. I once read that, "The mind once stretched by a new experience is never the same again." My knowledge and experiences have been forever altered and enhanced by the thesis journey. In addition, my family, friends and colleagues who had accompanied me on the journey vicariously enjoyed both the end of the journey and the re-entry to my home land.

Tips for Travellers in Thesis Country

I offer these suggestions for fellow travellers in thesis country in the hope that they can be helpful to you on your journey.

- ***Remember that the thesis is a process and not just a product.*** Although you are embarking on a research and writing task, remember that the process of writing your thesis in terms of planning and choosing your topic, choosing your committee, and conducting the research itself involves a lot of time and involves you personally. Your transformation by the thesis process is a very powerful one and cannot really be predicted in advance. What can be predicted, however, is that the thesis task and process will require a lot of your own personal time and energy. It would probably be helpful for you to begin discussions with family, friends, and work colleagues about how you would like to organize yourself during the thesis writing process, and ways in which, you think, they might be able to help you.

- ***Remember that the thesis is just part of your life, and not your whole life.*** Although it may seem like it at times, your thesis and your thesis journey are really only part of your whole life during your thesis writing phase. It is important to attempt to keep your life in balance through some "time outs" for relaxation, friendship. . . and fun! Thesis writing and the research process is hard work. If you are going to be able to pace yourself to complete the research process, you will need to find ways to recharge your batteries in whatever ways are most effective for you. What is important is that you find a way to keep the thesis in perspective. Remember that one day, the thesis will be over and you need to reconnect with your family, friends and the world.

It is helpful if you have been making attempts at doing this throughout the thesis journey.

- ***If you begin to feel overwhelmed by the work involved in your thesis, identify a series of small steps that you can accomplish and ways of recognizing each accomplishment.*** The thesis journey is a long one, but really only consists of a number of individual steps forward. Therefore, although the scale of the thesis journey seems large, it is possible to break it down into manageable, bite-size steps — ones that can be accomplished in a day, week, or month. Then, when you have completed a certain aspect of the thesis journey, such as deciding on your topic, having your proposal approved, or having completed your data collection, build in opportunities for celebration, once again, with family and colleagues. Everyone needs to understand the progress of your journey, and you need the opportunity to experience the feeling of progress — you are moving forward. Besides, it is more realistic to plan for the small steps, since most of us do not have the luxury of doing nothing else but thesis writing!

- ***The thesis journey is expensive... plan for it and budget wisely.*** The entire task of writing your thesis involves a lot of resource expenditure, both in terms of dollars and time. It is truly amazing how quickly the cost of photocopying can add up, and, if like me, you need to travel, tape-record and word-process to complete your thesis, additional costs are involved. If you have the opportunity to seek funding for your research, all the better. If not, then it would be worthwhile, in my opinion, to take out a personal loan to provide you with the financial security to be able to continue with the thesis process. This could be considered as an investment, as the cost of going on the journey.

In addition to the financial costs, the personal time, energy and commitment necessary for your thesis journey may necessitate your either delaying the process until you have the time to do it, or, realistically, planning your research itinerary so that the time constraints you have can

be built into your research design. Otherwise, the research will provide one form of challenge while your time
commitments will add additional degrees of difficulty to the
task.

If I Were A Guide

I believe that one of the reasons I had a positive thesis
journey was that my travelling companions were both
knowledgeable about, and sensitive to, the research process. Because of the "foreign" nature of the thesis process to
most new travellers, it is beneficial to have people accom-
pany you who have been on this journey before. There is
nothing like experience to help you understand and appreciate the "pitfalls" and summits of thesis country. Therefore, based on my own experience, these are the activities
that were most effective for me:

- *The thesis journey is front-end-loaded; choosing
  the itinerary is the most important part.* I believe that the single most important aspect of the
  thesis process is the determination of the best "fit"
  of topic for the traveller and the context. The importance of sharpening the focus of the traveller and
  clarifying the intention of the research project cannot be overemphasized. In addition, it is also important to explore the time constraints and availability of the traveller in determining the topic. The
  reality that the traveller also has a life outside of the
  thesis journey is important to remember, and the
  ways in which the thesis journey relates to that life
  need to be explored with potential travellers.

- *Be sensitive to and respectful of the "crises of
  confidence" of travellers.* If other travellers' experiences are like mine, there will be several times
  during the thesis journey when they will question
  their ability either to complete the task, or to embark on it at all. Although they may not express this
  directly, lengthy delays in completing proposals,
  delays between data collection and final analysis
  and delays in the defense process all are possible
  symptoms that there are affective challenges confronting your traveller. The part of thesis country
  that they are travelling on at that time may feel
  treacherous to them, and they need both your sensi-

tivity and respect if they are to navigate the narrow ledge successfully. Sometimes, bringing down the "scale" of the task helps, at other times, refocusing the task, and building in some short-term accomplishments might also assist the traveller. In essence, however, what is required is coming along side the traveller to reassure them on their journey and not rushing them or pushing them into territory alone which, to them, may feel frightening.

- *Keep the traveller moving forward. . . however slowly.* The thesis journey is a long one, and, from the beginning, looks almost too large to complete. Therefore, it is very helpful to travellers to give them small, concrete methods of continuing their forward progress. Some of the ways that were helpful to me to ensure forward progress included:

  a) establishing regular times to meet with my supervisor to describe and outline progress;

  b) agreeing on a project that had built-in time constraints which necessitated various aspects of the research being completed by certain dates;

  c) having a cohort of one or two graduate students working together to encourage each other along;

  d) noting and celebrating indications of your travellers' forward progress.

- *Consciously reflect on your own thesis journey and use your own experience, both in terms of the content and process of your thesis journey, to help you as a guide.* The opportunity of summarizing my experience has been extremely helpful in consolidating my own learning. It also makes me a better guide to others as they embark on their thesis journeys. It is often difficult to remember the challenging and negative aspects of the thesis journey once the final product, and the defense, have been formally completed. If you are to be effective and responsive to your travellers, therefore, it is helpful to review your own journey and to attempt to remember what it was like, what was helpful, what hindered your progression.

Riding a Roller Coaster in a Fog: Trusting the Search for Truth

Marian Pitters

Thesis Title:

**Health Care Educators in Transition:
How Peoples' Interactions Contribute
to their Learning**

Unpublished doctoral thesis, University of Toronto, 1991.

My study explored the process that occurs when people confront a significant change in their work and find the contributions of other persons to be important when making sense of their experience. The participants included both those who had experienced the change and those they identified as making the most important contributions to their meaning making. Using a qualitative approach I investigated three questions:

- Why do people get others involved in making sense of work changes?

- How do these people interact in this meaning making process?

- What are the outcomes of their involvement with each other?

Through interpreting the results, I developed a framework called the "dialogue of experiential learning," and practical guidelines for how people might use the framework when making sense of change.

"I hope you are radiating with pride and happiness." "I hope you savor the lovely feeling of success and completion." "Now what are you going to do with all your free

time?" These comments were typical of those written on
cards of congratulations that I received after successfully
defending my thesis. Although the words seemed very
appropriate for the occasion, none of them reflected the
immense relief that I felt upon finishing the multi-yeared
roller coaster ride of both confidence and doubt. This ride
found its home in my shoulders and bowels — either too
tight or too loose!

The roller coaster ride had begun seven years earlier. In
my first week at the university I learned from others with
similar time boundaries on their academic pursuits, that
you could "get out" a lot more quickly if you chose courses
that would support efficient completion of a thesis. Heed-
ing this advice, I tried to quickly focus on an area that was
of interest to me, to enroll in courses that addressed my
general interests, and then to define some questions I had
about that topic.

This very focused type of thinking meant harnessing my
natural tendency to entertain my limitless curiosity. A
wrestling match ensued wherein my drive to focus was
quickly dwarfed by my enthusiasm for an array of research
areas that presented themselves. These included world
peace, play, gerontology, and people who seem to be what I
called "powerful" or very competent experiential learners.
Over the next few months, a number of complementary
forces rekindled my drive for harnessing the exploration
and helped me to slowly converge on one topic. These
forces included: carefully choosing courses; writing term
papers; participating in learning partnerships; diving into
the literature; completing some pilot interviews; and, attempting to write a research proposal.

In a course entitled "Learning Values in Adulthood," I
realized by the second class that my search for a thesis
topic and my term paper had the potential to be synergis-
tic. This appealed to another natural tendency — my bias
for action. The process of writing a term paper, "A Values
Approach to Defining a Thesis Topic," was a catalyst for
my evolving understanding of: what is important for me to
research? and is it researchable? The document included
a number of both creative and rational strategies that I
had developed to enable my whole self to further define my
thesis topic and research questions. Sharing this work
with colleagues in our Adult Education department's Thesis Research Seminar, a number of people tried out some

of the strategies, and, subsequently, offered feedback on them.

By completing different exercises in "A Values Approach to Defining a Thesis Topic," my colleagues and I discovered ways to crystallize meaning and also to help others with similar interests. In this way we were moving into areas that had the potential to enter the realm of what Sullivan (1990) calls "emancipatory research," wherein we could struggle with a specific phenomenon in ways that were authentic to our own experience, and thereby come to know the possibility of freedom.

In addition to the synergy of writing a course paper, I discovered another force that helped me focus my topic in a class called Basic Processes of Adult Learning. Here we were encouraged to work with "learning partners," people with whom we met after class to discuss what went on within us as learners, and how we interpreted our experience of learning. Although we were invited to take time and get to know people before choosing our learning partners, I simply walked up to a person at the end of the first class who I thought would be fun and interesting. Thank goodness my first impression was accurate!

Our early morning weekly meetings were most enlightening, especially when I asked for some feedback about my search for a thesis topic. My learning partner's questions and comments challenged me to explore my own issues and strengths when making meaning with others, and, in particular, within the context of our partnership. Discussions quickly became a vehicle for both action and reflection. We tried out new ideas and strategies with each other and then processed how each of us made sense of what had happened in our meeting. Trust and openness evolved rapidly as we delved deeper into the essence of our meaning making processes.

Through discussion with my learning partner, I became more intimately acquainted with the roots of my search — that throughout my life I had enhanced my own learning when I got others involved in that process. Convinced that this was the top priority for my research, the frustration with considering too many topics ebbed away into an excitement of clarity. With growing confidence, I anticipated that writing my research proposal would be a breeze. Indeed the title and the introductory paragraphs were easy enough to formulate, but then the breeze blew in a flurry of

issues for my consideration. What specific questions did I
have about the topic? What made these questions important? Did other people have similar questions? Did they
think this area of research was important? What approach
would I use to answer these questions?

I pursued a variety of resources to find my way through
these questions. After a few intensive courses in adult
learning and in qualitative research, after months of discussions with other students and my thesis supervisor,
and after several weeks of poring over journals and books
in the coffee stained cubicles of the library, I started to
record questions that interested me the most about my
topic.

In the meantime, my first learning partner had returned
to his home town to write his thesis, so I became involved
with two other partners who were moving forward in the
thesis process. These two people had different but complementary perspectives that both resonated within me and
challenged me. I asked one of my new learning partners to
interview me on audio-tape using the questions I had been
developing.

The interview and subsequent reflections on that discussion thrust me up the roller coaster's steep climb and
wrenched me around some tight turns. I couldn't eat and
began to feel physically empty. I exemplified every adult
educator's favorite stinger of: "When you're churning,
you're learning." Jarred into a deeper realization of the
intellectual, emotional, and spiritual significance of this
kind of learning, I anticipated that the study participants
might have some sensitivity about discussing how they
involved others in making sense of their experience of
important changes at work. Reflecting further on this, as
well as the quality of answers on the audio tape, I made
some adjustments in the questions and developed some
plans about meeting with the participants.

I tested out these adjusted questions and new plans with
an educator who I knew was experiencing a great deal of
change in her work, or as she called it, "going through a
bad time." Upon completion of our interview, this colleague then arranged for me to interview the one person
whom had been most helpful to her. These two pilot interviews confirmed a number of hunches that I had, and they
established which questions would elicit the data that
would inform my study. The pilot interviews also brought

to light some new awarenesses about what I wanted to study and how I might do this. I had unwittingly accomplished what one professor had advised: "Set yourself up to be surprised."

With the pilot interviews completed, I returned to writing the thesis proposal. Scrounging around for guidance from other peoples' proposals, I thought: "Why hasn't someone written a handbook on how to write a qualitative thesis proposal? Why is it such a mystery?"

As I was writing and re-writing drafts of my proposal, I felt I was getting more concrete and specific, but making slow progress. One learning partner surprised me with small gifts at different stages that spoke to me of how this progress had different forms and energies: two painted wooden birds frolicked in the breeze of my window; a glass turtle caught the sunlight and shed rainbows of hope across the walls of the room where I worked; and a carved frog and an owl sat watching me . . . silently . . . waiting.

On the other hand, business colleagues, family, and friends began to question my student existence and future goals with: "What will you research?" "When will you be finished?" "What are you going to do with your degree?" I felt this weight of others' expectations keenly, but used its force to propel me forward in my progress. The questions became opportunities to practise articulating in one succinct sentence what I was researching. My proudest moments were when I could actually see understanding in others' eyes. My darkest moments came when people would nod, but I knew from their glazed over eyes that they either didn't understand, didn't care, or thought I had lost my mind!

As my proposal was taking shape, I developed some criteria for choosing the professors that would be on my thesis committee. My supervisor was an obvious choice within the adult education department simply because of my interests. But the other two members required more consideration. I had heard horror stories of how politics and disagreements among committee members had delayed certain students' progress. As this was a great fear, I formulated some questions to ask the people I was considering for the two openings.

- How do you like to work with students (e.g., see drafts, or finished product, etc.)?

- Would you be accessible if I got into trouble?

- What was your richest experience of working with a thesis student?

- What was your most repugnant experience?

- When are you going on study leave? sabbatical? Will you be available then?

- What are your current research interests?

- How do see my work relating to your research interests?

- Would you feel comfortable working with a feminist orientation?

- How do you feel about working with the other potential members of my committee?

- Here's why I'm considering you. (reasons) Are you interested in working with me?

After discussions with potential committee members, I double-checked with other students who had experienced the strengths that each of the three could bring to a thesis. I heard that one person was known for practicality and asking questions to stimulate critique. The second was actively investigating the area in which I was interested. The third was knowledgeable about various theoretical frameworks and how ideas relate. Knowing that my learning partners were strong on critique and that the literature was sparse on research in this area, I went with the last two. With this range of strengths, I was confident that I could access complementary kinds of guidance at different points in my journey.

Once my proposal was approved by my committee members, I began the work of research — identifying and interviewing the study participants. Based on the strong feelings that arose during my own interview, it was no surprise that one person I invited to participate refused, and one participant dropped out of the study. This was a delicate topic I was exploring and people potentially might feel very exposed. After each interview I solicited the participant's feedback on our meeting and made notes of my own impressions of the session. These notes helped me to immerse myself in the interviewee's world, in the interview itself, and in my own style and skill as an interviewer, thereby gathering data that I would not be able to glean from the transcripts alone.

Working with the transcripts was initially a routine and mechanical task of recording themes down endless page margins. It was quite a contrast to the energy that was generated in the interviews. I discussed my themes with one of my learning partners and integrated his perspectives and challenges. The study participants then reviewed the themes and edited as they saw fit.

Throughout this initial stage of analysis, the house was being renovated, and I was being interrupted with questions about the exact location of electrical outlets and the exact placement of skylights. Each of these very different types of brain activity, decision making, and naming, gave me a welcome break from the other. As I was reflecting on where the electrical outlets should be, I was also considering how to cluster the transcript themes in order to enhance my understanding of the original problem.

Through this clustering process I developed a framework of eleven categories which I soon found were too cumbersome and lifeless. I looked at other ways to cluster the data in order to eliminate overlap and enhance my understanding of the data. I was quite content to be in a fog, knowing that fog always breaks. I checked back again and again to: "what do I want to understand?", and pared down to six categories. I drew mind maps of the clusters, representing how they were linked. I quickly realized that I needed a lens through which to see the data — a point of departure from which to begin. As my work concerned understanding peoples' experience, I looked to Kolb (1984) and Hunt (1987) for a tool that could further facilitate the clustering of the data.

After taping multi-coloured flip charts all over the kitchen of one of my learning partners, I expounded over the drone of the dishwasher how the work of Kolb and Hunt had given birth to my new framework. The presentation was complete with musical and visual metaphors.   I knew I had piqued their interest when one asked the other: "Can you turn off the dishwasher? Its getting in the way of this." When I had finished and heard: "I think you've broken the back of this thing," from one learning partner, and: "I think you've got it licked," from the other, I knew I was on the final downhill of the roller coaster ride.

I must have missed seeing a detour sign at the bottom of that hill. My aging mother moved to Toronto as her health began to deteriorate. Life does go on during the thesis journey! Visits, errands, conferences with medical personnel, and endless family telephone discussions meant that I would lose about eighteen months of time on my thesis. The insensitive question "when are you going to finish?" now evoked a variety of sarcastic comments in my mind as well as more serious doubts. Thankfully, I had never learned how to quit, only to plod along to the finish.

Recalling my original discussions with committee members, all had said that they didn't like it when students would disappear for semesters at a time and then submit voluminous drafts with requests for speedy reviews. They liked to be kept up-to-date and forewarned of when work would be submitted. Off to my committee members went cards acknowledging most holidays with short explanations of my unfolding family situation, my turtle-like progress, and my anticipated future activities.

During that agonizing thesis slowdown, a moment arrived that felt like melt down. One of my learning partners announced he was quitting his thesis work. My heart sank to the basement. I tried to convince him that he was so close and should continue, and then realized I was saying that more for my need of support than for his need to get on with other priorities in his life. I felt the terror of abandonment, even though he committed to meeting with me to the end. The old doubts resurfaced. When would I ever find time to complete this?

After Mom's death I plunged back into the thesis with renewed vigor. "Time to finish," I thought as words poured onto the computer screen, line after line. Each evening, week-end, and holiday (after I tucked my daughter into bed much earlier than her friends), I closed my computer files for my consulting practice, pointed the arrow to the folder called "thesis," and clicked twice.

Writing up my findings proved to be easier than I had anticipated. As usual, I had several ideas about how to begin, the chapter titles, what I would write, and how I would write it. Surprisingly, the decisions flowed almost effortlessly and enjoyably, as did the writing. I tried to begin at chapter one and go in some kind of logical order, and ended up doing that part of the time. I purposefully did things to underwhelm myself with the task, such as adjusting my schedule so that I was writing during my high energy times of the day. On good days, I also trusted that "it will unfold, it will pull together."

Upon completing each section I sent drafts to my two learning partners. One had a minimalist's eye for eliminating excess and was quite cerebral, while the other was more emotive and requesting more detail. I recall one of our meetings where one's comment about a paragraph was: "Spare me; get out the violins"; a striking contrast to the other's comment: "Hey, I really like that! It speaks to me!" Somewhere between the two I discovered and trusted my own voice. I was living exactly what the study participants had assisted me in understanding — a phenomenon called a hermeneutic circle. People reading my thesis now, who know me more as a friend than as a student, say it sounds just like me instead of like traditional academic writing. Through the contributions of my various learning partners, the thesis committee members, and this task of completing a thesis, I have been true to and have discovered more about the integrity of my own voice.

The preceding paragraph was to end this description of my thesis journey. But in reviewing it, one of my learning partners suggested: "People will probably be interested in how your defense went. Are you leaving that out for any reason?" Clearly the defense was an important few hours, and I was shaky even though each of my committee members had assured me that I was well prepared. The thought that over six years of work could be wiped out in a few hours put me on edge. The large square table established an immediate formality that was contrasted by peoples' informal styles. The questions were respectful of the work and focused more on how I would envision the study being used in the future rather than challenging how I had completed the research itself.

Perhaps the feeling of anti-climax after the defense was a result of experiencing far more intense peaks and valleys over the years leading up to this event. After all, this marked where the roller coaster came to rest, and I could finally graduate from the ride.

Tips to Travellers
- Trust in God, but tie your camel.

- Tune in to be in tune.
- Trust your own process.
- In separateness is connection; in connection is separateness.
- Make your thesis your job; make your family your life.
- If you work and have a family, there's always evenings and week-ends.

If I Were a Guide. . .

- I would see myself as learning and traveling with each traveller.
- I would make available practical resources on the "how to's" of all stages of a thesis. These would include various proposal formats, strategies for getting started — both creative and rational, how to manage mental blocks, how to get affordable administrative assistance, tips from graduates, etc.
- I would invite students to provide feedback on how my guiding has been, and could be, most useful to them.
- I would encourage travellers to find learning partners, and to keep journals about their meetings.
- I would drop a few lines to students who hadn't been in touch, to indicate my caring.

What's It All About, Alfie?

Ellen M. Regan

Thesis Title:

The Relationship Between Teacher Beliefs, Teacher Classroom Verbal Behavior and Experts' Views of Selected Child Development Principles

Unpublished doctoral dissertation,
State University of New York at Albany, 1967.

My thesis research was, if nothing else, prophetic. Twenty-seven second grade teachers were observed twice during periods of classroom instruction. Selected verbal behavior derived from selected Child Development principles were recorded on an observation guide by trained observers. Teachers then responded to a questionnaire assessing the extent of their agreement with these Child Development principles and corresponding statements of teacher role. Appropriate statistical treatment and judgments of elementary education experts were used to establish the reliability and validity of these measures. Analysis of observation data (behavior) indicated that the 27 teachers revealed the same pattern with respect to the verbal behavior measured. Teachers' responses to the questionnaire indicated a high level of agreement with the Child Development principles and statements of teacher role (beliefs). Comparisons of beliefs and behavior, however, indicated contradictions that support the claim of gaps between educational theory and classroom practice. The common pattern of behavior was consistent with other findings regarding nature and range of teacher behavior.

The years since the completion of my research have been marked by a continuing search to understand what it is that explains how teachers and other professionals go about their work, especially their work with young children. The notion of "beliefs" has been central to these efforts. I am still wrestling with the what and how of professional beliefs, but I am satisfied that I have taken giant steps over these years in the way in which I have been exploring. Thus, I remain on a journey but, along the way, I have been privileged to guide the journey of some less experienced travellers who, in turn, enriched my continuing travels.

"What's It All About, Alfie"

Whenever I hear that song, my thoughts return to my thesis travelling days when that melody was among the top ten, my small apartment was littered with thesis stuff and my mind and heart were echoing what Dionne Warwick was asking Alfie, that is, What's it all about? The "it" in that instance was the whole experience of being a graduate student immersed in the thesis process. And immersed I was!! Even now I can appreciate how this process dominated my life whenever conversation turns to a discussion of the Viet Nam War, and I have difficulty keeping up with what is being said. Certainly I am old enough to remember this war but, in the mid 1960s, all of my attention was focused on getting a proposal accepted and, then, completing the thesis. My life and the thesis were one.

I think (and hope) I have carried the memories and lessons of my "travelling" days to my years as a guide. You need to travel before you can guide. You need to have travelled *that* road, to know the twists and turns, side roads, possible detours and, most of all, to know what it's like, how it feels to be traveller and why anyone starts this journey in the first place, that is, What's it all about? As a guide I have found this question useful at three particular points or stages of the thesis journey: (1) What is a thesis about? (2) What is this thesis about? (3) What is the whole experience about? These three questions relate, in turn, to understanding the nature of the task, understanding the specific task and "hanging in" when the task seems unending.

The Nature of the Task is . . .

As a rule, producing a thesis is, at most, a twice in a life time experience (i.e., master's and/or doctoral thesis). Perhaps a thesis is being completed by someone somewhere every minute of every day, but it is difficult to argue that it is a life experience repeated again and again for the individual. It is a new experience and most likely a one-time experience. Perhaps this is why would-be travellers often approach the exercise with much uncertainty and trepidation. Guides need to recognize the "newness" of the traveller's experience and appreciate his/her concerns.

The advice, "Go to the library and browse through some theses" may be a good suggestion but provides insufficient guidance for most travellers. Before the trip to the library, some travellers need to know something about what a thesis represents — that it is more than just a long term paper and less than a magical document.

All travellers I have met come to the thesis task with "an idea" or "topic," though many aren't sure what to do with the idea or topic, where to go with it ... except they want to get there "without a lot of statistics" if possible. This cart before the horse thinking is so common among beginning travellers that I believe we guide-teachers must be doing something wrong. To get the horse before the cart we need to encourage putting the idea (or topic) on the shelf, temporarily, and thinking about what research is, what researchers do. If the beginning travellers were as oriented to the notion of research as "finding out" as they are anxious about research methods, the early days of the journey would be less stressful. I am indebted to the guide who suggested to me, as a beginning traveller, that if I asked the right questions, I could always find the means of answering them. "What would you like to find out on this journey?" may be a guide's best input to the initial meeting with a traveller. This question can open the door to an exchange of ideas and experience that sets a context for the journey ahead.

Once when lost during a first visit to a small city, I stopped the car and asked a child, about five or six years of age, if he could tell me where Lee Street was. He looked at me in disgust and said "Everybody knows where that is." Guides should be careful not to assume that "everybody knows" what thesis research is or what it entails. This is a new city for many travellers who may need some time to get oriented.

The Purpose of This Thesis is . . .

Experience as both traveller and guide suggest that defining what "*this* thesis" is about is one of the more difficult tasks in the enterprise. A thesis "idea" is not useful until it is clearly spelled out in a declarative English sentence (or declarative structure in any language). Such spelling out is essential for determining the value of the idea, its potential for answering the implicit/explicit questions and the feasibility of the research. Some travellers I have known perceived the construction of a purpose (or intent) statement as an easy task and were annoyed when asked to put pen to paper and compose the sentence. Confident of the ease with which intent or purpose could be stated "later," these travellers were more concerned with the "real" work of getting subjects and selecting measures. Guides who do not discourage the latter before purpose/intent is clear do a disservice to travellers. It must also be recognized, however, that the successful spelling out of purpose or intent is preceded by considerable traveller reflection and dialogue with guides and other travellers. It is born after much mental tossing around until it comes together to produce the "aha" ... I know of no other way to describe it. Certainly there is input from many sources (e.g., literature, discussion) to this germinating process but it is what the traveller does with the input that makes the thrust, or the purpose, of the work uniquely his or hers. As travellers wrestle with the task, it may be useful to remind them that there can be beauty and strength in simple, clear, precise prose. The incomprehensible is not usually profound!!

What's This Whole Experience All About?

The whole thesis experience is about ups and downs, highs and lows, the camaraderie of fellow travellers and a heck of a lot of hard work. There is nothing magical about the process or the prize. From observations as both traveller and guide it seems to me that those who "drop out," who are ABD (all but dissertation) forever, are those who opt for other priorities ("This may be my last chance to go to Antarctica") and other ways of spending their time ("I want to finish my cottage in the Adirondacks"). Those who "hang in" have made a commitment to themselves to finish and are willing to postpone or put aside other experiences and to give their time and energy to the thesis. Certainly the support of family, friends and guides is important but only the individual traveller can complete the task, that is, the thesis buck stops there. This is why I often ask beginning travellers to think about why they want to take this journey, anyway. Unless there is the desire and commitment to "do" it for yourself, to meet the challenge you set, I'm not sure that the delayed rewards, inviting as they certainly are, will be enough to sustain any traveller.

As noted, I think the whole experience is also about the special relationship that develops among fellow travellers. It isn't just the pat on the back or help in chasing down a reference or a sympathetic ear that creates such soul mates; however, it is difficult to put a name to that intangible that travellers give to each other. I believe guides need to encourage travellers journeying down the same road to share with and nurture and laugh with each other. There is nothing like a little irreverence for all things (and people) academic to put things in perspective. I often forget the name of journal articles and books when I need the reference but I have never forgotten "The teaching of golf through audio visual aids to disadvantaged gifted students in the middle school." That was George's contribution to our round table at a local pub when we decided to define theses topics that, because of timelines and faculty interests (or passion), were sure to be approved. We needed that little exercise at that time and I think all travellers can profit from the occasional chance to look at where they are and what they are doing with a somewhat satirical eye. A thesis is certainly serious business but taking oneself and the process so seriously that there is no pause for a little perspective taking can make the journey doubly difficult. What's it all about, Alfie and Alice and Susie and Henry and . . .?

It's about a special time in your life, special people, and special problems. It's about a special journey that you would never choose to repeat, perhaps, but that you are really glad you took.

The Map is Not the Territory

John Weiser

Thesis Title:

A Study of College of Education Students Divided According to Creative Abilities

Unpublished doctoral dissertation,
University of Missouri, 1962.

Assisting students through the trials and tribulations of the thesis process has been a major part of my professional life for over twenty-five years. I believe I have learned something about this fascinating work by my own trials and errors and by observing the experiences of the many students with whom I have been associated during my career. I am, therefore, pleased and challenged by this opportunity to share some of my experiences and learnings.

Good Beginnings
My experience with my own thesis supervisor was a very positive one and certainly set me on the path of attempting to provide similar experiences for those with whom I have worked. As I recall, I felt very inadequate to the task of creating a thesis; however, with my supervisor's assistance, I broke the process down into small steps, set deadlines, persisted, asked for help when needed, paid attention to feedback, and finished within the time limit that I had set for myself. Quite naturally, I assumed that everyone could follow these simple guidelines and successfully complete their degree requirements in a reasonable period of time. I have since discovered that this is not always the case. Trying to understand what is blocking the progress

of each traveller (doctoral student) and finding a way to help in each situation has made the work of guiding (supervising) a fascinating, sometimes frustrating, and, in most cases, a highly rewarding enterprise.

When I began my doctoral research there was a fairly prescribed methodology available for almost any research question. Of course, one had to learn what was a research question within the confines of the accepted methodologies of the day. Once this requirement was satisfied, a researcher usually followed a well-established path to its conclusion. This process was particularly true of research conducted for the purpose of meeting the requirements for a degree. There is much of value to learn within this type of task; however, guiding a traveller along this path was seldom fun or stimulating for me and, I have little doubt, for the traveller as well. In fact, it was more often a terrifying experience for both of us.

It seemed to me that there was a lot to learn and, although each step along the way was fairly prescribed, there were a number of skills to master. These included learning to write in an acceptable style, designing the study, analyzing and presenting the data, and, of course, learning to correctly apply all the rules of grammar and the style rules of the American Psychological Association. It was my assumption that every good guide was an absolute master of everything. Knowing that I was not and trying to pretend that I was, set me up for the terror that I experienced. Working within a research model that seemed to imply that there was a right way and a wrong way to do everything and that any slip-up doomed the entire effort to failure helped neither the travellers nor myself to work in a relaxed or confident way.

The only acceptable solution for me was to be honest from the beginning with any potential traveller about what I believed were my particular strengths and limitations. I would then discuss with the traveller how these might be relevant to the traveller's proposed topic and design. I also encouraged travellers to assess themselves in the same way. By doing this early in the process, it sometimes became clear that the potential traveller and I made for a poor match in relation to our skills. Discovering this early allowed for a timely decision to be made as to whether we should work together or not. This is perhaps the most important choice that travellers and guides will make.

A Major Shift

Perhaps the most significant event in my experience as a
guide occurred when I began to learn about qualitative
research. With the help of some of my colleagues and
students at The Ontario Institute for Studies in Education,
a support network was formed to learn and promote research from this new perspective. As a result, my whole
attitude changed toward research in psychology, and I
began to enjoy the work of guiding. It would be difficult to
overstate how important this change in approach to research was to my professional life.

The most exciting difference for me was in the type of
research questions encouraged in a qualitative approach
(particularly heuristic) compared to a quantitative approach. One essential feature for me is that the questions
asked in a qualitative approach explore people's experiences, and a researcher's fundamental task is to attempt
to understand and capture those experiences. Naturally,
this implies that a researcher's own capacity to understand becomes central to the process. Thus, who the
researcher is becomes as relevant to the study as who the
participants are. Just as the research changed to a focus
on people as individuals rather than on abstract group
norms, so my work as a guide focused on the travellers as
whole individuals rather than on concentrating almost
solely on their technical skills as researchers. My comments on guiding will focus now on some of the most significant and potentially difficult situations I have experienced working with travellers following the qualitative
approach.

The expanded range of research questions being explored opened up the opportunity and necessity for a wider
range of design approaches. More often than not, these
approaches were created to fit the situation and were
subject to revision throughout the process as the researchers learned and responded to new information. Now, flexibility of guidelines for research became the norm and
justifications for design decisions could be related much
more closely to the situation and context of the research,
which changed the whole nature of a research proposal.
First, the original proposal becomes more tentative and,
secondly, it is required that the traveller and guide monitor
design and methodology issues on an ongoing basis.

In this book we are using the metaphors of guiding and

travelling for the tasks of thesis supervisors and doctoral candidates. By the use of these terms we are implying a journey in which a guide is familiar with the territory that a traveller must traverse. Let us extend this metaphor a little further. One possible arrangement might be described as that of travellers hiring a guide to lead them through unfamiliar territory in order to reach a goal. Travellers want a guide who has made the journey before, preferably many times, and can take them safely to the goal without any unnecessary delays and as few difficulties as possible. My image of this type of arrangement is that of travellers attempting to step as nearly as possible in the footsteps of their guide. The traveller's objective is to stay on the path or trail that the guide sets because it is considered dangerous to stray from this path. Both travellers and guides hope and intend to avoid any surprises along the way. The "map" the guide offers is like a road map through a territory. Thus, travellers learn about the road map and what can be viewed from a well-travelled road, but not much more about the territory through which the roads cross. It is this version of the guide-traveller metaphor that I associate with the more traditional research methods of the social sciences. I call this version, "The map is the same as the territory."

The Map is Not the Territory

The version of the guide-traveller metaphor that I associate with the new qualitative methodologies in the social sciences I call, "The map is not the territory." Here we have an experienced guide who is somewhat familiar with a vast territory and knows about some convenient roads or paths; however, the territory is relatively unexplored and no roads exist into vast parts of it. It is also important to point out that a map is only a poor approximation of some portion of reality. I mean to emphasize in this case that the word "territory," implies concrete reality.

Guides do their best to provide a crude map of the territory showing existing roads and topological features, while travellers decide what part they wish to explore regardless of the availability of roads. Since many travellers choose to go where there are no roads, they are required to make their own. Guides provide general information about what is known about the territory and some useful guidelines for creating new trails in this type of terrain. There is no emphasis on following another's footsteps in this version of the journey. Travellers are there in the reality of the territory by themselves and must choose each direction and each step themselves. Travellers learn from each step and its consequences and, thus, each moment provides the opportunity for surprises to occur. In fact, the journey is about being surprised and challenged and responding creatively. In this version of the metaphor, I see guides and travellers connected by radio or a wireless telephone. Also, a helicopter is available to fly travellers out and back at any time for rest and consultation.

In the first version, travellers are permitted to make one or two brief excursions off the beaten path. In the second version, travellers may return to the established path from time to time but they are really encouraged to create their own path. Their story is about their experiences and about the trail they have created and mapped. As a result, knowledge is gained about previously unknown territory.

I would like to offer some specific suggestions for a guide who identifies more with the second version of the journey and within a research paradigm that is appropriate for this approach. I have already mentioned several ideas that I consider important. I hope my suggestions will have relevance for guiding in general, as well as for this particular type of journey.

It is the Traveller's Journey. This is the most important principle for me. Another way of saying this is that the thesis belongs to the student. This implies that travellers choose the territory, and it is the reporting of their adventures and discoveries that make up the heart of the thesis. Over-identification with the thesis on the part of the guide commonly reduces the likelihood of a successful and exciting result.

Being Open to Originality. A guide must be prepared for and supportive of methodologies developed by travellers which will have unique features relative to their particular thesis. In addition, the guide needs to be respectful and supportive of a writing style that is personal and, therefore, appropriate for the particular journey and traveller. This style will be useful because the task of integrating methodology, strategies of presenting information, and personal meaning must come across to a reader as a whole piece.

This is dependent upon the traveller's ability and freedom to share and report on the process and meanings developed throughout the thesis.

Supporting Choice Making. In general, it is the guide's task to support travellers with potentially useful hints, and to share knowledge of other options for various choices that will occur throughout the entire process but, above all, the guide must keep reminding travellers that it is really their choice. It certainly helps to indicate faith in their ability to make appropriate choices. Among the most important requirements for a successful thesis and defense are being aware of choice opportunities, making choices, and justifying these choices in a reasonable way. Giving time and support at some of the crucial choice points seems to be one of the most useful ways that a guide can be of assistance. The consequences for travellers of working through these issues and making choices which best suit their work can be astonishingly positive. Travellers' assessments of themselves as writers, thinkers, and researchers have sometimes changed so dramatically from negative to positive over the course of the journey that it leaves little doubt about the worthwhileness of the project.

Getting Clear from the Start. I want to turn now to some ideas that I have found to be of use at the early stages of the work, specifically at the pre-proposal stage. Many times I have conferred with potential travellers who have come to me with a general topic in mind for a thesis but who seem to be rather vague about what or why they want to pursue these particular topics. I have often asked such students to bring me a list of all the questions they have about the topics they are considering. I encourage them to include both theoretical and personal questions in the list. This list is for them, not for me, and it is requested with the hope that it will help focus and clarify why this topic will be worth exploring. I have found it to be very useful to ask students to explore the question, "What are you curious about in relation to the topic?" I would pursue this further by asking, "What difference will it make for you to satisfy your curiosity?" As for the last question, I would spend some effort looking at how this would be useful to further knowledge in the field, as well.

It is also very useful to assist potential travellers to

explore their own assumptions and hypotheses about potential thesis topics. Often, the lists generated by the above questions provide a fruitful beginning for this work. In pursuing a qualitative approach, I suggest that all assumptions, hypotheses, and even previous research and theories be considered as biases that can be potentially dangerous to the success of a research project. In terms of the metaphor, travellers may not be able to really see the territory unless they are looking through naive eyes. Actually, the most successful journeys I have witnessed have been those where travellers have been able to switch from perspectives of naive and expert within themselves and also have been able to approximate the perspectives of others.

Releasing Creativity. I have found it useful and, in some cases, a key to releasing the creativity of travellers to approach this task of preparing a proposal from two different perspectives. The one perspective might be called the left brain approach. Here the questions and/or hypotheses generated are largely based on previous readings and research in the area, and the research questions are largely extensions from this body of material. The right brain approach calls for the exploration of the personal and intuitive, which are largely based on previous personal experiences of travellers and, thus, offer a clear opportunity for their emotional and non-rational ideas to come to light. Often travellers will find a slightly different direction for their work than that gained from the left brain approach as they become clearer about *their* motivations and the *real* basis for their curiosity. A sense of risk-taking very often begins here. It is important to note that if the thesis is to work it is this continuous interplay of the traveller's intuitions, hunches, and logic that will make it so. By the guide starting early to support and encourage these aspects of the traveller, the tone and general nature of the guide-traveller relationship are being communicated. This early support will also emphasize the respect the guide holds for the whole person of the traveller and the necessity for all of the person to be included if the work is to be successful.

In order to facilitate more of the intuitive nature of travellers, I have suggested that they spend some time each day for a week meditating about their proposed topic. I share with them a form of meditation in which they are asked to focus their awareness on anything that occurs to their consciousness. They are encouraged to notice what emerges and to take notes about anything that occurs; such as thoughts, images, sensations, and emotions. They are instructed to let go of negative and self-critical experiences as soon as possible and to return to their awareness again. It helps to review the notes made previously before beginning each day's meditation. If some particular aspect of a previous meditation appears interesting, it can be useful to focus this new period of meditation on this more specific aspect of the more general topic.

I have often suggested that travellers allow an image to appear in their mind, during their meditation, that represents the topic that they are considering pursuing. Later, we explore this image together for possible clues and meanings that are contained in the image. Since an image is, by its nature, a whole complex of meanings and relationships, exploring an image for the relationship of one aspect to another often will reveal an understanding about a topic that is not readily visible when simply listing separate ideas. It is often out of these activities that a clear focus for the thesis topic emerges as well as the motivational energy for the work, which is so necessary to sustain the project to its conclusion.

Trust the Traveller's Sense of Rightness. From my perspective, a thesis proposal, even after having been formally approved by a committee, must always be treated as a tentative plan. What is tentative are the number and demographics of the research participants, the style and content of the interviews and other research generated materials, and the analytical procedures which a traveller utilizes to handle the data. In some cases I have even supported a rather major shift in the basic research question of the thesis. These revisions emerge out of the ongoing experiences of travellers. The best preparation for dealing with the need for revisions comes out of the traveller's solid grounding in the philosophy and methodology of this type of research. How the need for revisions is recognized and dealt with is often a major aspect of the guide's and traveller's journey together.

In almost every case in my experience, it is the traveller's, rather than the guide's, sense that something is wrong or not working that initiates consideration for a revised direction. Within our metaphor, it is the travellers who are actually in the territory, and it is their experience which will indicate dissatisfaction with what is occurring. It is, therefore, a necessity that they learn to trust their own reactions to the work and to share this information with the guide. What may emerge at these times is that travellers blame themselves for the work not going well, rather than recognizing that the difficulty they are experiencing is useful information and a part of the essential nature of the territory itself. Assisting travellers in working through some of these times is often difficult. By indicating that I trust their sense of difficulty as being both appropriate and useful and, in addition, that I have faith that the best way to deal with the situation will emerge out of their creativity, has proven to be the most useful and rewarding approach for both of us.

One of the more interesting and exciting experiences in guiding for me has been when I feel certain that travellers have determined or recognized that the thesis is really their own, accompanied with the sense of the ability to do it. Witnessing this switch from travellers looking to experts for advice, direction, and responsibility for the thesis' success or failure, to one of ownership and sense of personal expertise has always been a thrill for me as a guide. Following this switch, travellers may continue to bring in just as many or more problems and difficulties to discuss but the situation becomes very different. For instance, in contrast to previous meetings, now travellers seem to express little fear that they will be able to work things out satisfactorily.

It is at this point that I try to focus on what the travellers may know, think, feel, hunch, or imagine. I do this because travellers are now so immersed in the material that they almost sense the problems organically. The solutions to difficulties can now emerge out of this mix of personal intimacy with the territory and the struggle to solve the difficulties. Travellers now seem to possess an internal trustworthy judge to whom they can refer to determine if their work is satisfactory and whether potential solutions to difficulties are acceptable. They seem to develop a solid and dependable sense of "rightness." This internal judge is also the source of recognizing difficulties or a sense of "wrongness." It has often been the case that travellers now become much more perfectionist about their work than they had been previously. In my years of guiding, it has proven very important to recognize this switch and to honor it.

Trust Your Own Sense of Rightness When It Comes From as Personal a Place as That of the Traveller. Several consequences of this switch in perspective on the part of travellers has been repeated in my experience. One is that travellers' newfound confidence, creativity, and flow of ideas can be so satisfying to them that they may temporarily lose some capacity to judge the work. More particularly, they may lose perspective on the relationship of their new ideas to the overall project. The task of guiding at these moments for me is to decide how to raise this type of issue and, yet, retain the overall relationship of support and respect for the traveller's work and experiences. The one principle that I have embraced is to keep my response personal. That is, I try to say what I am thinking and feeling in as straightforward a manner as I can. Included in my response should be the sense of respect and excitement or appreciation for the creative step that I see having been made. What is called for here is to express my own self-respect as well, not as an authority or from a power position but simply as me. There is a risk of this type of response being misinterpreted, but respectful honesty seems to have the best chance of being heard and considered at these times.

A second consequence that often occurs is that the experience of finding their own voice, of ownership, of experiencing a strong moment of personal creativity and insight into the phenomena under study can leave travellers with such a strong positive sense of gratification that they may believe that the main work of the thesis is finished. This is seldom true in my experience, and, once again, a potentially difficult moment exists between the traveller and the guide. What is usually called for, once again, is to assist travellers to relate these new ideas to the rest of the work. Also, it is often the case that these new ideas or insights raise as many questions as have been answered by this new perspective. It takes time and distance to be able to see this. Again, I suggest that the principle of speaking personally and honestly be followed. I will report to travellers what my questions are, relate how my curiosity has been aroused by this new perspective, and suggest how this curiosity can be satisfied. There is a very important matter of timing here that I have learned the hard way. Travellers must have the time to experience the joy and gratification of their creative experience and, even better, to be joined in this celebration. Introductions of new directions, or suggestions of possible limitations of these new ideas cannot be heard or understood, and certainly are unappreciated if made prematurely. Each situation is unique. I have learned, however, that I will most likely err by going too fast. It is hard to overemphasize the degree of anger and resentment that can be aroused at these times on the part of anyone whose new creation has just been stepped upon or seen as diminished in any way.

This principle of waiting for the sense of completion to occur and the gaining of some distance and a larger perspective to again become available before moving on also applies to the writing of the final chapters of a thesis. In my experience, drafts of final thesis chapters are almost always written from a narrower perspective than the previous chapters would warrant. Here I see the need for the guide to encourage travellers to sit with the material for a while. There are some activities that travellers can do at this time to assist them in formulating their approach to the final phase of their work. I will often encourage travellers to review all of their early questions and how they located their study in the field, in order to see where the study has taken them in regard to the proposal stage of the study. Sometimes I have found it useful to suggest to travellers that they now attempt to identify what has been the most surprising feature of the study or what they consider to be the most important feature of the work in relation to theory, practice, and future research. Consideration given to these issues has provided some sense of direction and a focus for travellers' thoughts at this time and has resulted in the presentation of some excellent ideas and interesting perspectives on the overall implications of their experiences.

I believe that I, as the guide, can be very helpful here in counteracting the rush to finish that so often is the case. I will try to indicate to travellers my feelings about the positive progress that has been achieved and follow this up by sharing my sense of the potential for something even more exciting to emerge than has occurred up to now. Some-

Keep On Trekking: It Is Exciting!

Linda Williams

Thesis Title:

Developmental Patterns of Teaching Careers

Unpublished doctoral thesis,
University of Alberta, 1986.

I needed a change. I had started teaching 15 years earlier. Not all those years were full; few had been in the same school or grade more than twice. In talking with my skiing and squash buddy over dinner one evening, I decided to apply for a sabbatical to begin the doctorate program in which I had been accepted the previous year. I had chosen the program because I was interested in the work of an individual at the university, the reputation of the university was good, and, I could afford to go there.

Happily, I was granted sabbatical and my plans proceeded! By the end of the school year, I was so exhausted that, as I enjoyed the mountain lifestyle of Kimberley, British Columbia, I seriously considered becoming a ski bum and forgetting the sabbatical, the doctorate, and teaching in general. Again a friend helped by suggesting that since I had this opportunity, I might as well continue. I could quit teaching afterwards. This was the first of many times when I seriously considered abandoning my goal, a friend or family member would help keep me going.

That summer was the best of my life, leaving me well prepared for Graduate Studies. I was rested and had an excellent perspective on the next passage. As I was enthusiastically describing my summer adventures, the one woman I knew at the university showed more than the average interest in my tales. No, she did not want to see

the pictures, but did I like music (Yes) and did I like kids
(Yes). Well, she had a friend who liked to hike and ski and
had just bought a condominium in Kimberley. He had
four kids and liked music. His wife had died two years
before. Did I want to meet him? With a nonchalant agreement, my doctoral travels took on an additional dimension.

The journey began when I registered for my first semester. My plan was to complete all the class requirements in
one year and the thesis in the next. All doctoral candidates at this university were required to take the same four
classes in the first semester. To encourage the support
network, our offices were clustered in the same room.

We were a motley crew from different parts of the globe
and with varied experiences. I was surprised, initially, at
the number of us who were there because we needed a
change. We wanted to earn our degrees but not at all
costs. Somehow, this group was able to keep the process
in perspective. Professors indicated that our wholesome,
supportive comradeship was unique among doctoral
groups. We did our part to build cohesiveness by making
music together at weekend parties. (The widower played
guitar.) Everyone seemed to sense this was a special time
set apart from our regular lives. We worked hard *and* had
fun.

I had entered the program with a plan to examine teaching behaviors and/or patterns of teachers' careers. While
teaching with the Faculty of Education, I had noticed the
theories I was teaching were more useful to me in the
classroom than they were to my students, and, my students would return after a stint in the classroom and say,
"Now I understand what you were saying." Two approaches
proved very helpful: I often used my professional experiences as topics for class assignments and further study,
and usually I turned assigned papers into background
reading for a possible thesis whenever practical. As a result, a considerable portion of my literature review was
completed before I began the thesis.

One of the thrills of doctoral study was reading the work
of others who had come to the same conclusions that I had
derived from my own experience. I was right! Then, when
necessary, I could find someone to quote in support of my
inside-out theories. At one point I wondered if there were
any new thoughts and encountered one of the challenges
of determining your research topic!

The timeline proceeded, hurried by my upcoming marriage and my desire to finish. My thesis supervisor was a pragmatic person, and, together, we set out a schedule. Early in the second semester, we agreed on the thesis topic and began assembling a thesis committee. With his experience in the department, my supervisor knew in whose field my interest lay and which individuals would be "good" to have on my committee politically and academically. We looked for those who would do the job well, and, without unnecessary delays.

The choice of supervisor is critical. You want someone whose work you respect and in whose area you want to study. Someone who has done similar work will be able to understand your goals and coach you as necessary. You want someone who will challenge you to help you think and grow but not to be difficult; one who will be rigorous but not tedious; and one who does only what needs to be done and leaves you to travel on your own as much as possible. A supervisor who carries weight in the department is very helpful: you do not want to have to jump hoops for the sake of jumping hoops. Nor do you want someone who had a difficult time as a graduate student and so believes all those following should suffer.

I chose a supervisor who had published work which interested me. With his breadth of experience in research, his political and academic astuteness, and the respect with which he was held in the department, his approval of research topics and designs made acceptance by other committee members quite secure.

My supervisor allowed me freedom to work on my own, but did not abandon me. He asked the right questions to keep me on track or challenge me to look with a different view. He recommended certain theses and books for me to read both as background information and as examples for style.

During this process, the thesis of a colleague was particularly intimidating. I read it and thought two things: he had done it all and I would not ever be able to write something so perfectly! Having recognized and accepted that fact, I proceeded.

My very last class was held the day I married and became mother of four. I missed the class. The date set to defend my proposal before my committee was three days after I returned from my honeymoon. "You are ready. You just won't have time to get worried," had been my supervisor's comments. Besides, I had to have my proposal approved in order to collect the data before the school year was over!

Thus it was. My husband and I returned to Calgary from the Caribbean on Sunday. I had one day with our four children and left for Edmonton on Tuesday. Wednesday was my candidacy. My plans were approved and I was a doctoral candidate!

Immediately arrangements had to be made to interview thirty teachers as soon as possible and find a sitter for our five-year-old. At the same time, I was learning how to be Mother and run a large household. One day when I picked up Peter, who was five and who had been my child for only a month, he said, "Now I know how long three hours is. She said you would be back in three hours." It does not take long to feel guilty about leaving small children, I concluded!

Juggling between Kindergarten and babysitters, making suppers and cleaning house, driving to soccer and music lessons, I was able to collect my data by June 13. I understood what women live through! For the rest of June, I could just be Mom with the exception of a few letters and phone calls to complete this stage. My supervisor and a colleague jokingly suggested I should write my thesis on the transition to Mom.

The data analysis stage began with the purchase of our first computer because the $5000 investment was cheaper than hiring a typist. Having believed I could not think and write without my pencil, I was not sure whether I could write with a computer. Thankfully, I could, even through the process of learning two word-processing packages! There was the frequent dilemma of whether to spend time to learn something new in order to save time down the road, or to do it quickly the old way. The investment of time to learn always paid off.

Transcribing the tapes began during the summer. The "aahs" and fuzzy words were frustrating. Expediency and self-preservation won: the typed transcript was accurate enough. One cannot worry too much and finish a doctorate.

Once the school year resumed, I was student from 8:30 a. m. until 3:30 p.m. and Mom before and after, with some overlap. By October 31st, all the tapes were transcribed and the analysis began! My questions had led to certain themes, but comments from the teachers identified others.

The transcribing, analysis, writing, and adjusting to being wife and mother were difficult and trying times. It was a lonely time, one simply requiring a stick-to-itiveness which came from deep within, bolstered by the help, love and support of friends, family, my supervisor and my faith. Many times I was ready to leave either or both projects! I had scriptures and friends on whom to hang in those moments of fear, doubt, panic and all three. I began to think universities granted doctorates to anyone who survived.

Thankfully, with the approval of my supervisor, I had written the first three chapters in quieter times before collecting my data. As a result, the labor of the remaining chapters was manageable. I was in contact with my supervisor by telephone and infrequent trips to the university.

As I neared completion, one of my committee members, the President of the university, asked how I was feeling. I answered, "like I'll never finish, like I wrote the wrong thesis and like I missed the point!" He said it was normal. Later, a discussion with a respected colleague in Toronto about my study caused me to look at my work from a new perspective. I would have written it differently if I had talked with him earlier. But, given the time (the thesis was done, the oral defense date set), I decided to proceed as planned. I could continue the exploration after I had finished.

The thesis was like a birth: ideas had a gestation period through which I just had to live. No matter the agony, I simply could not make it move ahead of its time. As well, the writing assumed a life of its own, simultaneously being shaped by, and shaping, external forces so that the end result was different than anticipated.

The help from unexpected sources and situations surprised me. Discussions with moms while we watched our children at their swimming lessons or soccer games, gave me tremendous insights into my study. Simultaneously, I was amazed that the situation for me as new mom, learning my role, was parallel to the one for teachers learning their jobs. Comments on their career developments reflected my experience in my new career and helped me know "it was okay."

At times, the words would just not come out, or, would

come out jumbled. I learned tricks to use on myself. "It's okay to begin in the middle." "No editing until the end of the sentence!" "No, sit down and keep going." Or, I would wander, eat or drink, and, with the change of scenery, would find the words.

Finally, on October 31, 1985, it was all over. I defended my thesis and was finished. What an incredible feeling! I literally felt taller. (How can that be? I know they talk about the "monkey on your back" and being "weighed down" by something, but really!) I was so excited to be able to read anything I wanted to read just because I wanted to read it. I did not have to read anything. The fact that I had attained that doctorate, the highest degree and the one my professors had, was awe inspiring. There was a sense, too, that I had finished, that that's all there was. At the same time I knew, of course, there was more to learn and do.

My doctoral journey was a special time, a time of ecstasy and agony, of new friendships and new directions. My life did change but not as I had anticipated in becoming Assistant Superintendent for my school board. I virtually have left teaching, but the PhD has opened doors and enabled me to move in new directions and begin new journeys. I enthusiastically encourage friends and colleagues to take the step: it is a worthy struggle and it feels good.

Tips to Travellers

- Stay with a favorite aunt who thinks you are wonderful, will feed you well and otherwise spoil you.

- Have an idea of what you want to research and use assignments for background reading.

- Your supervisor is the most important choice you make.

- Life will dictate the parameters within which you will have to work as much as, or more than, will your research design.

- Your research is a living thing formed by you and your environment.

- Slow down brain. There is only so much I can do.

- Do not edit until you have finished the sentence.

- You can start in the middle.
- Finish for the sake of finishing. There is life after thesis and you can do it all then.
- One cannot be perfect and finish a doctorate.
- They give doctorates to those who survive.

If I were a guide
- I would have fun suggesting topics of research.
- I would encourage my students with questions and attention.
- I would remove all the barriers possible to free up the student for the drudgery and fun of their work.
- I would only pick committee members who are interested in aiding the student's journey.
- I would encourage my students to keep a journal of all their thoughts, questions, doubts, ideas, and joys.

Final Reflections

Ardra L. Cole and David E. Hunt

When these separate reflections came together, they
formed a book with life of its own, an inquiry into the
thesis process which exemplified the doctoral thesis itself.
It yielded many themes about the thesis process specifically and human affairs generally with many more variations from a myriad of viewpoints. Therefore, although we
had not originally planned to do so, we conclude with a
very brief synopsis of some of the major themes.

Whether the research is a doctoral thesis or another
investigation, inquiry into human affairs is a part of the
human venture. Accordingly, the activities of travellers and
guides on the thesis journey are as revealing of human
affairs as are the more formal results of the thesis. The
thesis journey is a part of the human journey, and no
attempt to objectify or depersonalize the process can deny
this connection. As George Kelly stated in his Reflexivity
Principle (1955), both travellers and guides are a part of
the phenomenon they seek to understand, and they must
include themselves in the account of the inquiry. The
thesis journey is mightily influenced by the beliefs held by
travellers and guides about the nature of human affairs
and especially the nature of knowing.

Travellers and guides who accept their own humanity
and the central role of persons-in-relation in human affairs
are both liberated and challenged. Travellers who accept
that their thesis journey emanates from their own deep
values and beliefs experience many benefits. By beginning
with themselves, they build a foundation for their inquiry
based on their own experienced knowledge. By opening

themselves to their senses and perceptions, they gain access to more meaningful understanding of their topic. By accepting the reciprocity of mutual learning between themselves and their research participants, they can both document the importance of persons-in-relation as well as opening themselves to personal development.

Guides also benefit from acknowledging that they, too, are participants in the human venture they seek to understand. They become more aware of their assumption about the nature of knowledge and how we accrue knowledge. By adopting the maxim, "Teaching is learning, learning is teaching" they open themselves to developing by travelling on their own related journeys. By contrast, they also learn that the journey finally belongs to the traveller, and that to respect this ownership is ultimately the most facilitating role of the guide.

As noted in the Introduction, there are still many areas of social science which insist that researchers must control, if not deny, their humanity, by becoming detached impersonal observers. As noted by several of the guides in recounting their days as travellers, such false obeisance to this image of the Scientist in the White Coat only brings restriction and impoverishment in understanding. For inquiry into human affairs, we can never learn more than our assumptions about the nature of human affairs permits. If we take on the role of detached observers and treat our participants as subjects, then we can only learn about the human condition when the participants are under highly controlled, restricted conditions.

Perhaps the most frequent themes dealt with how the traveller related to or was connected with the various parts and persons in the thesis journey. First, how do travellers relate to themselves, how do they understand their own beliefs about inquiry and the nature of knowing? How do these beliefs play out in their actions? Next, what is the travellers' relation to their topics? Is it dear to their heart, is it a passionate connection? The relation between travellers and topic is vital to the central feature of commitment and its role in thesis completion.

The relation between traveller and guide, i.e., candidate and supervisor, was emphasized in almost every reflection. This relation is so vital that it needs to be clarified, negotiated, and continually considered by both parties. The relation of traveller to participants is of serious importance, especially since this relation signifies the travellers' beliefs about the possibility of relational knowing. Participants cannot be truly collaborators because the thesis is ultimately the traveller's responsibility, but the relation can be maintained as open, reciprocal, respectful, and as mutually beneficial as possible. Perhaps less apparent, but nonetheless important, is the traveller's relation to other travellers, i.e., engagement in research teams or support groups. Travelling together was a common theme which facilitated the journey for many travellers.

The theme of balance occurred frequently, and nowhere was this more important than in relation to the traveller's family, those nearest and dearest. Often this relation requires not only balance and negotiation, but continual re-negotiation. Finally, there is the relation of the travellers to their own development and change as they move along on their journey. Are you prepared to change and develop? Are you prepared to revise some of your basic beliefs? Are you open to surprise? All of these attitudes are central to the possibility of the traveller's growth, development and increased understanding as a result of the journey.

We have been emphasizing commonalities and similarities, and in the final theme we turn to the uniqueness of each individual journey. This is an application of experiential learning to the doctoral thesis: travellers must learn through their own direct experience with their journey even if others may have travelled a similar path before. It seems that where human affairs are concerned, not only does each generation need to learn for itself, but so too does each person. Accepting this necessity is especially important for guides who may feel at times that this territory has been mapped earlier. It is important to acknowledge earlier inquiry, of course, but partly because of the nature of how each of us learns from our own experience, this principle is very important. To state that each journey is unique raises questions about the cumulative nature of knowledge about human affairs, an issue which every traveller must address.

We did not intend with this book nor with this final section to answer all the questions, rather like any valuable inquiry we hope that it has stimulated the reader, provided a variety of viewpoints, and exemplified how inquiry into human affairs can rejuvenate those who engage in the inquiry and those who read about it.

References

Berlin, I. (1992, May 28). "Philosophy and life: An interview," *The New York Times Review of Books* pp.46-54.

Blanchard, K. (1984). *Situational leadership II*. San Diego, CA: Blanchard Training and Development, Inc.

Braithwaite, B. (1988). *Teachers as persons, theorists and practitioners.* Unpublished doctoral thesis. University of Toronto.

Britton, J. (1977). *Language and learning.* Harmondsworth: Penguin.

Collingwood, R. G. (1958). *The principle of art.* London: Oxford University Press.

Diamond, C.T. P. (1991). *Teacher education as transformation: A psychological perspective.* Milton Keynes: Open University Press.

Diamond, C. T. P. (1993). Inservice education as something more: A personal construct approach. In P. Kahaney, J. Janangelo, & L. A. M. Perry (Eds.), *Teachers and change: Theoretical and practical perspectives.* New Jersey: Ablex Press.

Diamond, C. T. P. & Zuber-Skerritt, O. (1986). Postgraduate research: Some changing constructs in higher education. *Higher Education Research and Development,* 5(2), 161-174.

Ely, M. et al. (1991). *Doing qualitative research: Circles within circles.* London: Falmer Press.

Flam, J. D. (1993). *Matisse on Art.* New York: Phaidon Press.

Griffin, G. B. (1992). *Calling: Essays on teaching in the mother tongue.* Pasaden, CA: Trilogy Books.

Heaney, S. (1980). *Preoccupations, selected prose 1968-1978.* London, UK: Faber and Faber.

Hersey, P., & Blanchard, K. (1982). *Management of organizational behavior: Utilizing human Resources* (4th edition). Englewood Cliffs, NJ: Prentice-Hall.

Hoft, B. (1982). *The Tao of Pooh.* New York: Dutton.

Hunt, D. E. (1987). *Beginning with ourselves: In practice, theory, and human affairs.* Cambridge, MA and Toronto, Ontario: Brookline Books and OISE Press.

Hunt, D. E. (1992). *The renewal of personal energy.*
Toronto, Ontario and Newbury Park, CA: OISE Press and
Sage.

Huxley, E. (1959). *The flame trees of Thika.* New York:
Morrow.

Kelly, G. A. (1955). *The psychology of personal constructs.*
Vols.1 & 2. New York: Norton (1992, second edition,
London: Routledge).

Kolb, D. (1984). *Experiential learning: Experience as the
source of learning and development.* Englewood Cliffs,
N.J.: Prentice Hall.

Lennie, I. (1993). Long quiet highway of the soul. *The
Globe and Mail,* July 28,
p. A.22.

McIntosh, P. (1985). *Feeling like a fraud. Work in progress*
(No. 18). Wellesley College, Wellesley, MA: The Stone
Center.

McIntosh, P. (1989). *Feeling like a fraud: Part 2. Work in
progress* (No. 37), Wellesley College, Wellesley, MA: The
Stone Center.

Nathan, M. (1961). *Virginia Woolf.* New York: Grove Press.

Nelson, V. (1993). *On writer's block: A new approach to
creativity.* Boston: Houghton Mifflin.

Rennie, D. L., & Brewer, L. (1987). A grounded theory of
thesis blocking. *Teaching of Psychology, 14,* 10-16.

Sarason, S. B. (1972). *The creation of settings and the
future societies.* San Franciso: Jossey Bass.

Sternberg, D. (1981). *How to complete and survive a doctoral dissertation.* New York: St. Martin's Press.

Sullivan, E. (1990). *Critical psychology and pedagogy:
Interpretation of the personal world.* Toronto, Ontario:
OISE Press.

Tolstoy, L. (1954). *Anna Karenin.* London, UK: Penguin
Books.

Wall, M. (1992). The centrality of self in women's learning
experiences during graduate study. Unpublished M.A.
thesis, University of New Brunswick.

Woolf, V. (1929). *A room of one's own.* NY: Harcourt Brace.

Contributors

William Alexander is an Associate Professor in Adult Education at OISE.

Eleanor Allgood is Principal of Rideau District High School in Elgin, Ontario.

Mary Beattie is an Assistant Professor at the Faculty of Education, University of Toronto.

Elizabeth Burge is an Associate Professor in the Division of Adult and Vocational Education, University of New Brunswick, Fredericton, New Brunswick.

Ardra Cole is an Assistant Professor in Applied Psychology at OISE.

Catherine Comuzzi is a consultant in Toronto, Ontario.

Patrick Diamond is a Professor in the Joint Centre for Teacher Development at OISE and the Faculty of Education, University of Toronto.

Laura Ford is a Visiting Scholar in Applied Psychology at OISE.

Dorothea Gaither is a consultant in Toronto, Ontario.

George Geis is a Professor in Higher Education at OISE.

Mary Hookey is an Associate Professor at Nipissing University, North Bay, Ontario.

David Hunt is a Professor in Applied Psychology at OISE.

Solveiga Miezitis is a Professor in Applied Psychology at OISE.

Donald Musella is a Professor in Educational Administration at OISE.

Margaret (Peggy) Patterson is Assistant to the Academic Affairs Vice President, University of Guelph, Guelph, Ontario.

Marian Pitters is a consultant in human resource and organizational development and a writer in Toronto, Ontario.

Ellen Regan is a Professor in Applied Psychology at OISE.

John Weiser is a retired Professor who worked in Applied Psychology at OISE.

Linda Williams is an organizational effectiveness consultant in Oakville, Ontario.